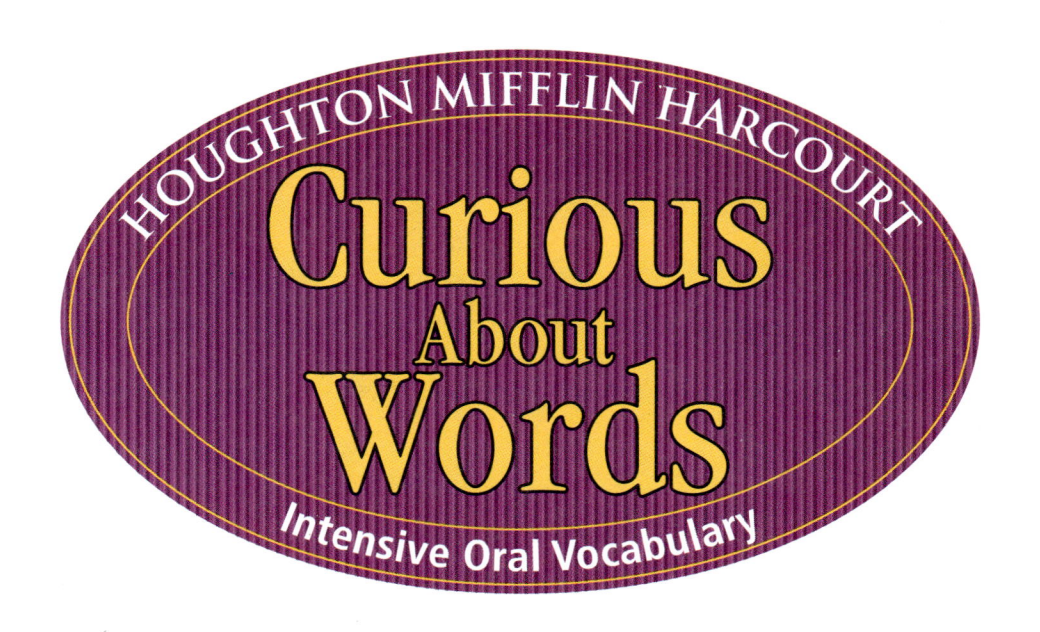

Curious About Words
HOUGHTON MIFFLIN HARCOURT
Intensive Oral Vocabulary

Teacher Manual
Grade K

HOUGHTON MIFFLIN HARCOURT
School Publishers

ILLUSTRATIONS

Illustrations © by Houghton Mifflin Harcourt Company/School Division. All rights reserved.
Cover illustration: Chris Lensch.

Copyright © by Houghton Mifflin Harcourt Publishing Company

All rights reserved. No part of this work may be reproduced or transmitted in any form or by any means, electronic or mechanical, including photocopying or recording, or by any information storage or retrieval system, without the prior written permission of the copyright owner unless such copying is expressly permitted by federal copyright law.

Permission is hereby granted to individuals using the corresponding student's textbook or kit as the major vehicle for regular classroom instruction to photocopy copying masters and test pages from this publication in classroom quantities for instructional use and not for resale. Requests for information on other matters regarding duplication of this work should be addressed to Houghton Mifflin Harcourt Publishing Company, Attn: Contracts, Copyrights, and Licensing, 9400 South Park Center Loop, Orlando, Florida 32819.

Printed in the U.S.A.

ISBN-13: 978-0-547-32746-4
ISBN-10: 0-547-32746-3

2 3 4 5 6 7 8 9 10   0877   18 17 16 15 14 13 12 11 10
4500238623

If you have received these materials as examination copies free of charge, Houghton Mifflin Harcourt Publishing Company retains title to the materials and they may not be resold. Resale of examination copies is strictly prohibited.

Possession of this publication in print format does not entitle users to convert this publication, or any portion of it, into electronic format.

Curious About Words
Grade K

How to Use *Curious About Words* **1**

Instruction

Unit 1

Lesson 1 .... **T2**
Mother Bear, Vol. 1
A Family Thanksgiving, Vol. 1

Lesson 2 .... **T4**
Learning to Swim, Vol. 1
A New School, Vol. 1

Lesson 3 .... **T6**
Runaway Hamster, Vol. 1
Dogs Like Stories!, Vol. 1

Lesson 4 .... **T8**
Family Chores, Vol. 1
Guide Dogs, Vol. 1

Lesson 5 .... **T10**
Amazing Ants, Vol. 1
The Sledding Accident, Vol. 1

Unit 2

Lesson 6 .... **T12**
Sounds Around Us, Vol. 1
A Day at the Beach, Vol. 1

Lesson 7 .... **T14**
Whale Songs, Vol. 1
The Mixed-Up Message, Vol. 1

Lesson 8 .... **T16**
Fantastic Gymnastics, Vol. 1
Animal Games, Vol. 1

Lesson 9 .... **T18**
What Does a Library Do All Day?, Vol. 1
Learning How to Build a Sandcastle, Vol. 1

Lesson 10 .... **T20**
Charles M. Schulz, Vol. 1
The Drawing Lesson, Vol. 1

Unit 3

Lesson 11 .... T22
Getting Ready for Winter, Vol. 1
A Favorite Season, Vol. 1

Lesson 12 .... T24
Tornadoes, Vol. 1
The Snow Day, Vol. 1

Lesson 13 .... T26
Humita's Plate of Colors, Vol. 1
How Stripes Protect the Zebra, Vol. 1

Lesson 14 .... T28
Amazing Penguins, Vol. 1
A New Home for Marvin Mouse, Vol. 1

Lesson 15 .... T30
Stories in the Stars, Vol. 1
Cloud Shapes, Vol. 1

Unit 4

Lesson 16 .... T32
Water on the Move, Vol. 2
A Special Bone, Vol. 2

Lesson 17 .... T34
Peaches and Bees, Vol. 2
What's in the Field?, Vol. 2

Lesson 18 .... T36
A Scavenger Hunt at the Seashore, Vol. 2
In One Big Red Bucket, Vol. 2

Lesson 19 .... T38
Hiking for Blueberries, Vol. 2
A Visit to Yosemite National Park, Vol. 2

Lesson 20 .... T40
Ferdinand Magellan Explores the World, Vol. 2
Exploring for Treasure, Vol. 2

Unit 5

Lesson 21 .... T42
Peaceful Pocahontas, Vol. 2
Moving Day, Vol. 2

Lesson 22 .... T44
Dinosaur Shapes and Sizes, Vol. 2
Little Puppy Learns to Be a Kitten, Vol. 2

Lesson 23 .... T46
From Ducklings to Ducks, Vol. 2
Growing Beans, Vol. 2

Lesson 24 .... T48
Clever Camouflage, Vol. 2
Amber and Olive, Vol. 2

Lesson 25 .... T50
Popcorn from Scratch, Vol. 2
A Harvest Feast, Vol. 2

Unit 6

Lesson 26 .... T52
Maggie's Big Day, Vol. 2
A Time to Help, Vol. 2

Lesson 27 .... T54
Too Little, Vol. 2
You're Never Too Young to Dial 9-1-1, Vol. 2

Lesson 28 .... T56
The Art Contest, Vol. 2
Walt Disney, Vol. 2

Lesson 29 .... T58
The Perfect Pet, Vol. 2
Michelle Kwan, Vol. 2

Lesson 30 .... T60
The Last Day of School, Vol. 2
Kindergarten Talent Show, Vol. 2

Assessment: Pretest/Posttest

Administration

Unit 1
Lesson 1	62
Lesson 2	63
Lesson 3	64
Lesson 4	65
Lesson 5	66

Unit 2
Lesson 6	67
Lesson 7	68
Lesson 8	69
Lesson 9	70
Lesson 10	71

Unit 3
Lesson 11	72
Lesson 12	73
Lesson 13	74
Lesson 14	75
Lesson 15	76

Blackline Masters

Unit 1
Lesson 1	92
Lesson 2	94
Lesson 3	96
Lesson 4	98
Lesson 5	100

Unit 2
Lesson 6	102
Lesson 7	104
Lesson 8	106
Lesson 9	108
Lesson 10	110

Unit 3
Lesson 11	112
Lesson 12	114
Lesson 13	116
Lesson 14	118
Lesson 15	120

Administration

Unit 4
Lesson 16	77
Lesson 17	78
Lesson 18	79
Lesson 19	80
Lesson 20	81

Unit 5
Lesson 21	82
Lesson 22	83
Lesson 23	84
Lesson 24	85
Lesson 25	86

Unit 6
Lesson 26	87
Lesson 27	88
Lesson 28	89
Lesson 29	90
Lesson 30	91

Blackline Masters

Unit 4
Lesson 16	122
Lesson 17	124
Lesson 18	126
Lesson 19	128
Lesson 20	130

Unit 5
Lesson 21	132
Lesson 22	134
Lesson 23	136
Lesson 24	138
Lesson 25	140

Unit 6
Lesson 26	142
Lesson 27	144
Lesson 28	146
Lesson 29	148
Lesson 30	150

Word List 152

How to Use Curious About Words

Intensive Oral Vocabulary Instruction

Curious About Words provides intensive oral vocabulary instruction for children with limited vocabularies in Grades K through 3. These materials supplement the core vocabulary instruction in *Houghton Mifflin Harcourt Journeys*. Daily lessons use read alouds, graphic organizers, teacher-led discussion, and partner activities to develop children's listening and speaking vocabularies.

In *Curious About Words*, a wide range of meaningful, useful words are taught each week in two semantic categories. Clear, student-friendly labels help children make connections between the categories of words. All words are drawn from research-based lists of high-utility words, including academic content vocabulary from Robert Marzano's *Building Background Knowledge*. For more information, see Research Sources for Words Taught on page 158.

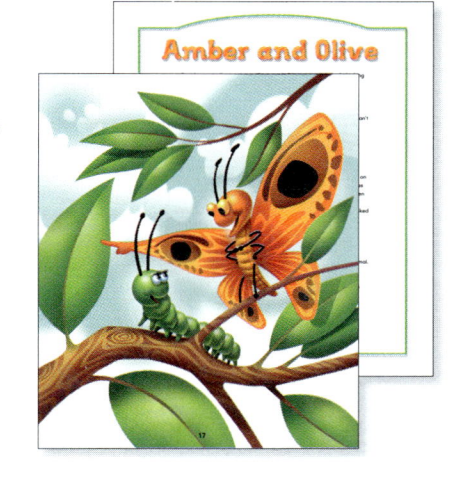

Read Alouds Two read alouds are the basis of instruction every week. Each read aloud introduces a new category of words. Every read aloud is accompanied by an appealing, full-page illustration or photograph, creating a collection of engaging narrative and expository texts. Oral vocabulary words are highlighted, and comprehension questions encourage discussion of the text as well as the oral vocabulary.

Daily Lessons Oral vocabulary is taught using student-friendly explanations and examples. Teacher-led discussions use graphic organizers to explore the relationships between the words in each category. Teacher-supported partner activities guide children to review and extend their understanding of all words taught in the week.

Assessments A single set of assessments is provided for each week, including the two categories of words. Each weekly assessment can support your instruction in two ways:

- **Pretest** Administer the assessment at the beginning of the week to determine which words children already know and which will require extra instructional time.
- **Posttest** Administer the assessment at the end of the week to determine how well children have learned the vocabulary that has been taught.

These assessments are administered orally to the group. Each has two components:

- **Pretest/Postttest Administration** Use this page to read aloud each item. In each item, the description after each circle corresponds to a picture, in left-to-right order, on the blackline master. Use these descriptions to name and discuss each picture (answer choice) with children. (Be careful not to reveal an answer.) 
- **Pretest/Postttest Blackline Masters** Copy and distribute each page. Explain that it shows only the answer choices. Help children understand how to circle the picture that best answers each question.

Unit 1
Lesson 1

Mother Bear

Days 1 and 2

"Mother Bear," Vol. 1, pp. 2–3

A Family Thanksgiving

Days 3 and 4

"A Family Thanksgiving," Vol. 1, pp. 4–5

Assessment
Pretest/Posttest Administration p. 62

Pretest/Posttest Blackline Masters pp. 92–93

T2 • Curious About Words

Day 1

Introduce Meanings

Assess To assess what word meanings children already know, copy and distribute the **Pretest/Posttest** on pages 92–93. Use page 62 to administer the test.

Explain Write each oral vocabulary word below on the board. Read it aloud. Offer an explanation and a brief example for each word.

Words About Moms

her *pron.* belongs to a girl or woman *The girl shared her snack with a friend.*

mother *n.* a woman who has children *The mother takes care of her baby.*

parent *n.* a mother or father *You need to go to the movie with a parent.*

she *pron.* a girl or a woman *My mom said she would read a book out loud.*

Discuss Guide children to see the relationship between each word and the category. Ask questions such as these: Which of your **parents** is a woman? What color is **her** hair?

Read Aloud Explain that you will read aloud a story about how a mother bear takes care of her cubs. Then read aloud "Mother Bear." Discuss the Comprehension questions.

Day 2

Categorize and Classify

Reread and Explain Reread "Mother Bear." At the end of each sentence that includes an oral vocabulary word, stop and repeat the explanation of the word. Then reread the sentence.

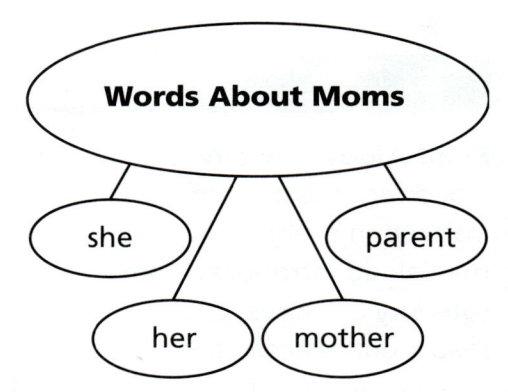

Use a Graphic Organizer Use the graphic organizer and the questions below to reinforce understanding of the relationship between each word and the category.

```
        Words About Moms
         /     |     \
        /      |      \
      she   parent
      /        |
    her     mother
```

1. What is another word for **mother**? (parent)

2. How does a mother show that **she** loves **her** children? (Sample answer: hugs them, spends time with them)

3. Name some things a mother does. (Sample answer: works at a job, cooks dinner, mows the lawn)

15-20 Minute Lessons

Unit 1

Lesson 1

Day 3

Introduce Meanings

Explain Write each oral vocabulary word below on the board. Read it aloud. Offer an explanation and a brief example for each word.

Words About a Family Visit

cousin *n.* a child of an aunt or uncle *My cousin Ben is my Aunt Cindy's only child.*

crowded *adj.* filled with people *The bus was so crowded that some people had to stand.*

food *n.* what you can eat *Pancakes are her favorite food.*

visit *v.* to go see *He will visit his grandmother over the weekend.*

Discuss Guide children to see the relationship between each word and the category. Have students think about a time when they **visited** other people in their family. Prompt them to use the words to describe what the gathering was like.

Read Aloud Explain that you will read aloud a story about a big family that is celebrating Thanksgiving together. Then read aloud "A Family Thanksgiving." Discuss the Comprehension questions.

Day 4

Categorize and Classify

Reread and Explain Reread "A Family Thanksgiving." At the end of each sentence that includes an oral vocabulary word, stop and repeat the explanation of the word. Then reread the sentence.

Use a Graphic Organizer Use the graphic organizer and the questions below to reinforce understanding of the relationship between each word and the category.

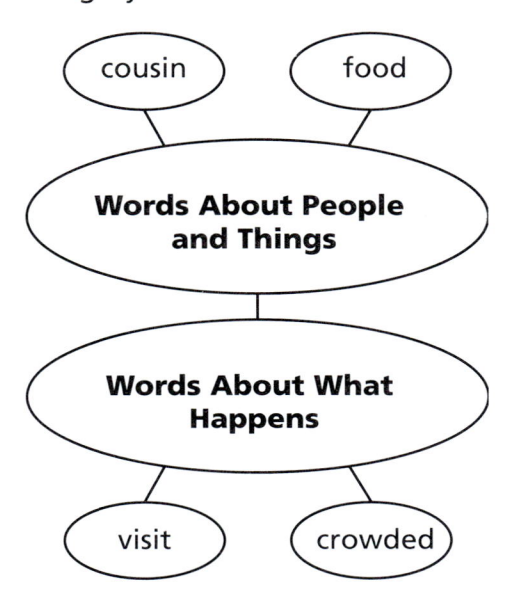

```
    cousin        food
        \         /
         \       /
    Words About People
        and Things
            |
            |
    Words About What
        Happens
         /       \
        /         \
    visit        crowded
```

1. What are some other words about who or what might be at a family gathering? Add these to the graphic organizer as children suggest them. (Sample answers: aunt; uncle; grandmother; grandfather)

2. What kinds of **food** does your family like to eat? Add these to the graphic organizer as children suggest them. (Sample answers: rice; chicken; spaghetti)

3. What word might you use to describe the classroom when all the children are in it? (**crowded**)

Day 5

Deepen Understanding

Review Repeat explanations for all oral vocabulary words. Use the definitions and examples from Day 1 and Day 3.

Guide Partner Activities Have partners work together to complete each of the activities below. Circulate and listen to partners as they work. Provide corrective feedback.

Examples Tell your partner about a time when you were in a **crowded** place. Tell what it looked like and how you felt.

Role-Play Work with a partner. Show what would happen if a **cousin** came to **visit**. Act out what you would do together.

Draw Draw a picture of you and a **parent** cooking **food** together.

Discuss Talk about all the things your **mother** does for you. Think of a way you could thank **her** for something **she** has done for you.

Assess To assess what word meanings children have learned, copy and distribute the **Pretest/Posttest** on pages 92–93. Use page 62 to administer the test. Compare scores with Day 1 assessment.

Unit 1, Lesson 1 • **T3**

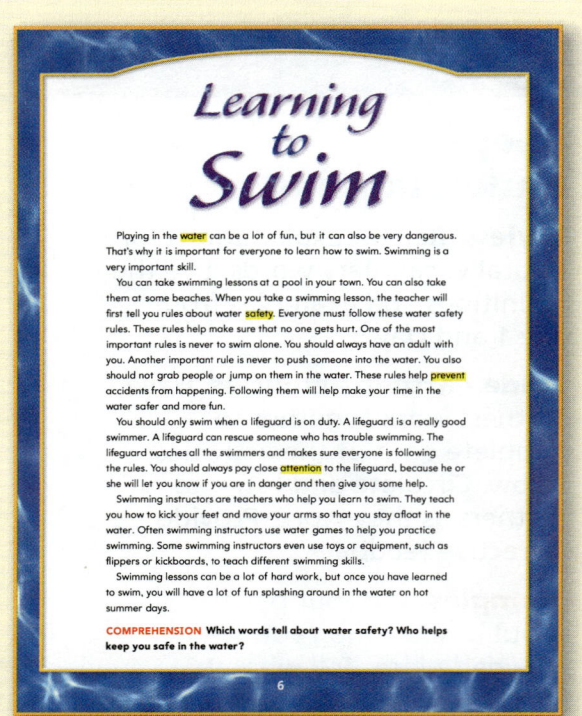

Unit 1
Lesson 2

Learning to Swim

Days 1 and 2
"Learning to Swim," Vol. 1, pp. 6–7

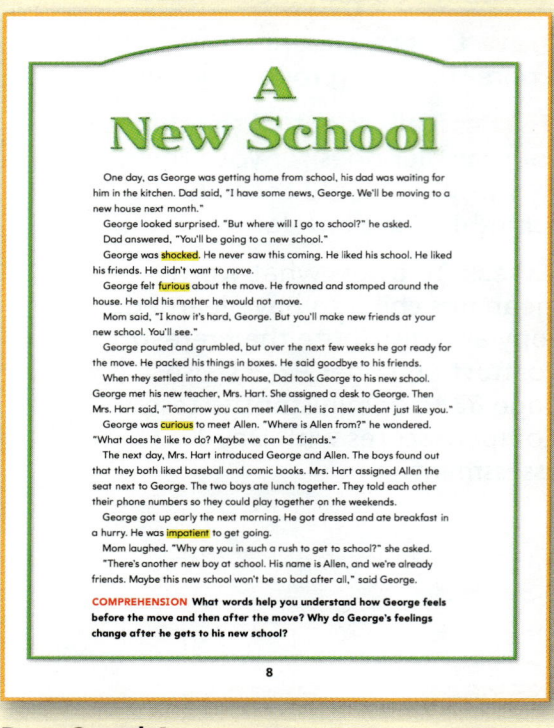

A New School

Days 3 and 4
"A New School," Vol. 1, pp. 8–9

Assessment
Pretest/Posttest Administration p. 63

Pretest/Posttest Blackline Masters pp. 94–95

T4 • Curious About Words

Day 1

Introduce Meanings

Assess To assess what word meanings children already know, copy and distribute the **Pretest/Posttest** on pages 94–95. Use page 63 to administer the test.

Explain Write each oral vocabulary word below on the board. Read it aloud. Offer an explanation and a brief example for each word.

Words About Being Safe in Water
attention *n.* watching, listening, and keeping in mind *Pay attention to what your teacher tells you to do.*
prevent *v.* to stop *A seat belt can prevent a person from being hurt.*
safety *n.* freedom from danger *Wear a seat belt in the car for safety.*
water *n.* a clear liquid *We drink water when we are thirsty.*

Discuss Guide children to see the relationship between each word and the category. Ask questions such as these: What can you do to **prevent** yourself from getting hurt in the **water**? What things should you pay **attention** to when you are in the water?

Read Aloud Explain that you will read aloud a story about how to stay safe when swimming. Then read aloud "Learning to Swim." Discuss the Comprehension questions.

Day 2

Categorize and Classify

Reread and Explain Reread "Learning to Swim." At the end of each sentence that includes an oral vocabulary word, stop and repeat the explanation of the word. Then reread the sentence.

Use a Graphic Organizer Use the graphic organizer and the questions below to reinforce understanding of the relationship between each word and the category.

```
        Words About Being Safe
         /         |         \
      safety    prevent    attention
```

1. When riding a bike, people should pay **attention** to _____. (Sample answers: other bike riders; people walking; cars)

2. What word might you use to describe what a lifeguard does at a pool? (**prevents**)

3. What are some things you can do with **water**? (Sample answer: swim in it, take a bath in it, drink it)

Unit 1

Lesson 2

15–20 Minute Lessons

Day 3

Introduce Meanings

Explain Write each oral vocabulary word below on the board. Offer an explanation and a brief example for each word.

Words About Feelings

curious *adj.* interested The <u>curious</u> kitten sniffed the new toy.

furious *adj.* very angry Marta was <u>furious</u> because her best friend didn't come to her birthday party.

impatient *adj.* not wanting to wait Greg was <u>impatient</u> to open his birthday presents.

shocked *adj.* surprised or upset She was <u>shocked</u> to find a snake in the yard.

Discuss Guide children to see the relationship between each word and the category. Prompt students to discuss how they would feel in different situations. Ask questions such as this: What would make you feel **curious**?

Read Aloud Explain that you will read aloud a story about how a boy feels when his family moves and he must go to a new school. Then read aloud "A New School." Discuss the Comprehension questions.

Day 4

Categorize and Classify

Reread and Explain Reread "A New School." At the end of each sentence that includes an oral vocabulary word, stop and repeat the explanation of the word. Then reread the sentence.

Use a Graphic Organizer Use the graphic organizer and the questions below to reinforce understanding of the relationship between each word and the category.

Words About Good Feelings	Words About Bad Feelings
curious	furious
	impatient
	shocked

1. Being **curious** is a good feeling. What other words tell about good feelings? Add these to the graphic organizer as children suggest them. (Sample answers: happy; excited; loving)

2. Being **furious** is a bad feeling. What other words tell about bad feelings? Add these to the graphic organizer as children suggest them. (Sample answers: angry; worried; sad)

3. Imagine you had to wait in a very long line to get your lunch. What word might describe your feelings? (**impatient**)

Day 5

Deepen Understanding

Review Repeat explanations for all oral vocabulary words. Use the definitions and examples from Day 1 and Day 3.

Guide Partner Activities Have partners work together to complete each of the activities below. Circulate and listen to partners as they work. Provide corrective feedback.

Categorize Work with a partner. Draw three things that make you feel **impatient**. Then draw three things you like to pay **attention** to.

Examples Describe a time when you felt **shocked**. Explain why you felt that way and what you did to show that feeling.

Role-Play Show how you might look if you are feeling **furious**. Then show how you might look if you are feeling **curious**.

Draw Draw a picture that shows a place where you could find **water**.

Discuss Talk about the rules for **safety** in the classroom. Explain why following the rules can **prevent** accidents from happening.

Assess To assess what word meanings children have learned, copy and distribute the **Pretest/Posttest** on pages 94–95. Use page 63 to administer the test. Compare scores with Day 1 assessment.

Unit 1, Lesson 2 • **T5**

Unit 1
Lesson 3

Runaway Hamster

Days 1 and 2

"Runaway Hamster," Vol. 1, pp. 10–11

Dogs Like Stories!

Days 3 and 4

"Dogs Like Stories!" Vol. 1, pp. 12–13

Assessment

Pretest/Posttest Administration p. 64

Pretest/Posttest Blackline Masters pp. 96–97

T6 • Curious About Words

Day 1

Introduce Meanings

Assess To assess what word meanings children already know, copy and distribute the **Pretest/Posttest** on pages 96–97. Use page 64 to administer the test.

Explain Write each oral vocabulary word below on the board. Read it aloud. Offer an explanation and a brief example for each word.

Words About Size
enormous *adj.* very big *The skyscraper is an <u>enormous</u> building.*
large *adj.* big *We need a <u>large</u> van to carry eight people.*
little *adj.* not big *The <u>little</u> cat sleeps on a pillow.*
small *adj.* not big *A mouse is a <u>small</u> animal.*

Discuss Guide children to see the relationship between each word and the category. Prompt them to use the words to describe objects in the classroom. Then ask: Can something **enormous** fit in your hand?

Read Aloud Explain that you will read aloud a story about a small pet hamster that goes to school in an unusual way. Then read aloud "Runaway Hamster." Discuss the Comprehension questions.

Day 2

Categorize and Classify

Reread and Explain Reread "Runaway Hamster." At the end of each sentence that includes an oral vocabulary word, stop and repeat the explanation of the word. Then reread the sentence.

Use a Graphic Organizer Use the graphic organizer and the questions below to reinforce understanding of the relationship between each word and the category.

Words About Small Things	Words About Big Things
little	large
small	enormous

1. What words might you use to describe an ant? **(little, small)**
2. What are some other words that mean **little**? Add them to the graphic organizer as children suggest them. (Sample answers: tiny; mini)
3. Why might an **enormous** dog scare people? (Sample answer: People might think the dog will knock them down.)
4. What are some other words that tell about **large** things? Add them to the graphic organizer as children suggest them. (Sample answers: giant; huge)

15-20 Minute Lessons

Unit 1

Lesson 3

Day 3

Introduce Meanings

Explain Write each oral vocabulary word below on the board. Read it aloud. Offer an explanation and a brief example for each word.

Words About Time

sometimes *adv.* now and then *The librarian <u>sometimes</u> reads a book to the children.*

soon *adv.* in a short time *<u>Soon</u> after packing her bag, she went on a trip.*

suddenly *adv.* quickly, without warning *Ben was asleep when <u>suddenly</u> the phone rang.*

until *conj.* up to that time *The class did not go on a field trip <u>until</u> the end of the year.*

Discuss Guide children to see the relationship between each word and the category. Prompt them to talk about their classroom schedule, using the words. Ask: What is something that will happen **soon**?

Read Aloud Explain that you will read aloud a story about how dogs are trained over time to become reading partners. Then read aloud "Dogs Like Stories!" Discuss the Comprehension questions.

Day 4

Categorize and Classify

Reread and Explain Reread "Dogs Like Stories!" At the end of each sentence that includes an oral vocabulary word, stop and repeat the explanation of the word. Then reread the sentence.

Use a Graphic Organizer Use the graphic organizer and the questions below to reinforce understanding of the relationship between each word and the category.

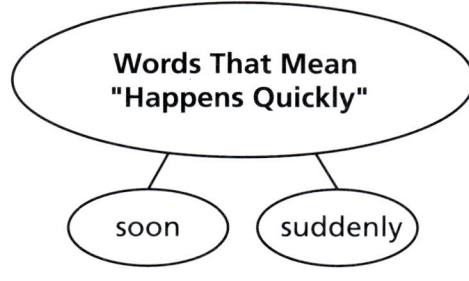

```
      Words That Mean
      "Happens Quickly"
         /        \
      soon      suddenly
```

1. What are two things that can happen **suddenly**? (Sample answer: rainstorm, fire drill)

2. What are some other words that describe things that mean "happens quickly"? Add them to the graphic organizer as children suggest them. (Sample answers: fast; speedy)

3. Name things that happen **sometimes** at school. (Sample answers: visits from guests; school concerts)

4. Why should you wait **until** the crossing guard tells you to go before crossing the street? (Sample answer: to be safe)

Day 5

Deepen Understanding

Review Repeat explanations for all oral vocabulary words. Use the definitions and examples from Day 1 and Day 3.

Guide Partner Activities Have partners work together to complete each of the activities below. Circulate and listen to partners as they work. Provide corrective feedback.

Examples What do people **sometimes** do at the beach or at a pool? Tell your partner.

Role-Play Show how you might pick up a **little** puppy. Then show how your face might look if the puppy **suddenly** barked at you.

Describe Talk to your partner. Describe something fun you are going to do **soon**. Tell how you feel about waiting **until** it is time to do that.

Compare Talk with your partner. Compare the size of a bear to the size of a rabbit. Use these words: **large, small**.

Draw Draw a picture of something **enormous**. Tell your partner about it.

Assess To assess what word meanings children have learned, copy and distribute the **Pretest/Posttest** on pages 96–97. Use page 64 to administer the test. Compare scores with Day 1 assessment.

Unit 1, Lesson 3 • **T7**

Unit 1
Lesson 4

Days 1 and 2
"Family Chores," Vol. 1, pp. 14–15

Days 3 and 4
"Guide Dogs," Vol. 1, pp. 16–17

Assessment
Pretest/Posttest Administration p. 65

Pretest/Posttest Blackline Masters pp. 98–99

T8 • Curious About Words

Day 1

Introduce Meanings

Assess To assess what word meanings children already know, copy and distribute the **Pretest/Posttest** on pages 98–99. Use page 65 to administer the test.

Explain Write each oral vocabulary word below on the board. Read it aloud. Offer an explanation and a brief example for each word.

Words About Helping Out

chores *n.* small things you do to help out *Her chores include making her bed and walking the dog.*

help *v.* to do something together with someone *He will help his brother pick up the toys.*

responsibility *n.* something that someone has to do *It is the baby-sitter's responsibility to watch the children.*

wash *v.* to clean with soap and water *Dad will wash the dishes after dinner.*

Discuss Guide children to see the relationship between each word and the category. Ask questions such as these: What are some **chores** you do at home? Does this **help** your family?

Read Aloud Explain that you will read aloud a story about a family who shares the chores in the house. Then read aloud "Family Chores." Discuss the Comprehension questions.

Day 2

Categorize and Classify

Reread and Explain Reread "Family Chores." At the end of each sentence that includes an oral vocabulary word, stop and repeat the explanation of the word. Then reread the sentence.

Use a Graphic Organizer Use the graphic organizer and the questions below to reinforce understanding of the relationship between each word and the category.

1. What can someone do to a dirty floor to make it clean? (**wash** it)

2. One **responsibility** a teacher has is _____. (Sample answer: helping kids learn)

3. Name some ways to **help** your teacher clean up the classroom. (Sample answer: put away books, throw away trash)

15-20 Minute Lessons

Unit 1

Lesson 4

Day 3

Introduce Meanings

Explain Write each oral vocabulary word below on the board. Read it aloud. Offer an explanation and a brief example for each word.

Words About Jobs

busy *adj.* full of activity The <u>busy</u> coffee shop had a long line of customers.

job *n.* the work that someone does The doctor's <u>job</u> is to help sick people feel better.

services *n.* work that helps others The school won an award for its <u>services</u> to deaf students.

work *n.* what someone does for a job He enjoys his <u>work</u> as a truck driver.

Discuss Guide children to see the relationship between each word and the category. Prompt them to use these words to talk about jobs their parents or other caretakers do.

Read Aloud Explain that you will read aloud a story about the job that guide dogs do. Then read aloud "Guide Dogs." Discuss the Comprehension questions.

Day 4

Categorize and Classify

Reread and Explain Reread "Guide Dogs." At the end of each sentence that includes an oral vocabulary word, stop and repeat the explanation of the word. Then reread the sentence.

Use a Graphic Organizer Use the graphic organizer and the questions below to reinforce understanding of the relationship between each word and the category.

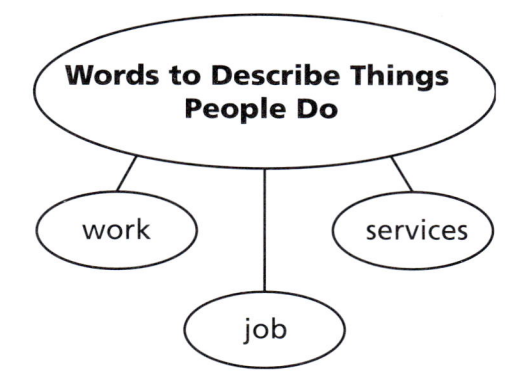

Words to Describe Things People Do
- work
- services
- job

1. Why is a firefighter's **job** dangerous? (Sample answer: A firefighter could get hurt.)
2. What word might you use to describe a fire station after the fire alarm rings? (**busy**)
3. Name two **services** that firefighters do for people. (Sample answer: put out fires, rescue cats from trees)

Day 5

Deepen Understanding

Review Repeat explanations for all oral vocabulary words. Use the definitions and examples from Day 1 and Day 3.

Guide Partner Activities Have partners work together to complete each of the activities below. Circulate and listen to partners as they work. Provide corrective feedback.

Compare Talk to your partner. Compare a **responsibility** you have at school to a responsibility you have at home. Use these words: **help, work, busy.**

Role-Play Take turns with a partner. Pretend you are a teacher. Name the **chores** you would ask your students to do. Your partner can act out each chore.

Examples Describe some **jobs** that a librarian does. Then name some **services** that a library offers to people. Tell a partner.

Draw Draw a picture showing how to **wash** a dog. Show your picture to a partner.

Assess To assess what word meanings children have learned, copy and distribute the **Pretest/Posttest** on pages 98–99. Use page 65 to administer the test. Compare scores with Day 1 assessment.

Unit 1, Lesson 4 • **T9**

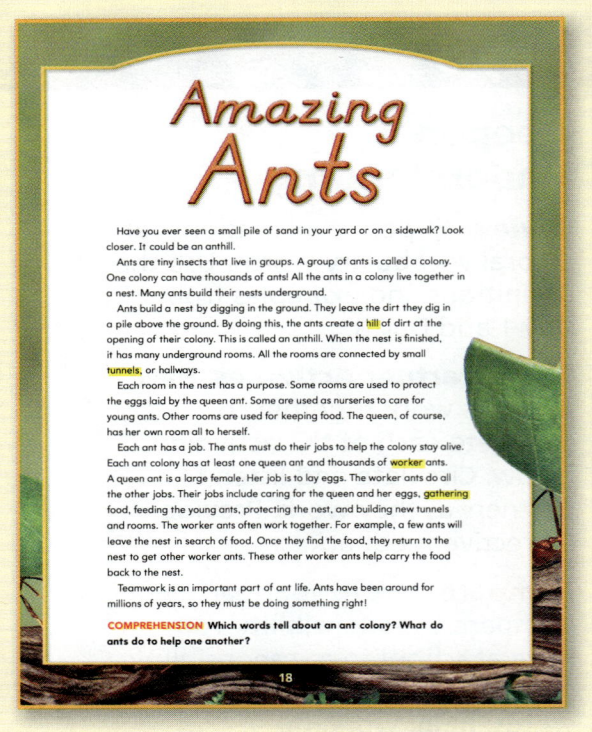

Unit 1
Lesson 5

"Amazing Ants"
Days 1 and 2
"Amazing Ants," Vol. 1, pp. 18–19

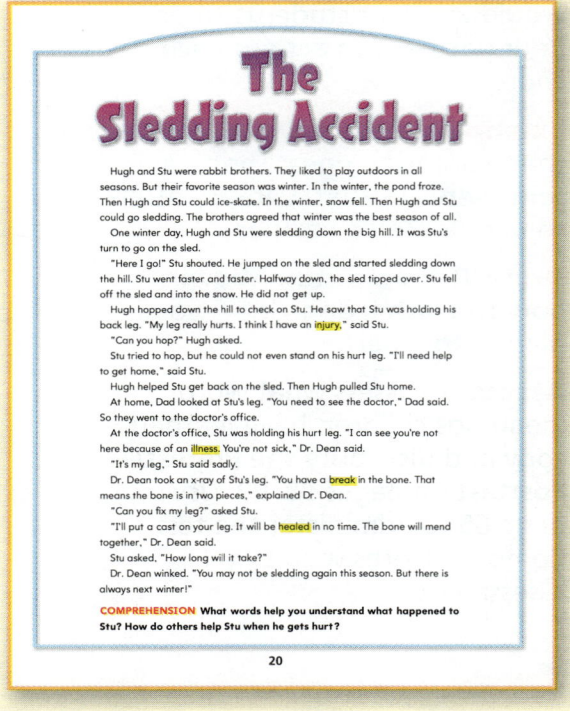

"The Sledding Accident"
Days 3 and 4
"The Sledding Accident," Vol. 1, pp. 20–21

Assessment
Pretest/Posttest Administration p. 66

Pretest/Posttest Blackline Masters pp. 100–101

T10 • Curious About Words

Day 1

Introduce Meanings

Assess To assess what word meanings children already know, copy and distribute the **Pretest/Posttest** on pages 100–101. Use page 66 to administer the test.

Explain Write each oral vocabulary word below on the board. Read it aloud. Offer an explanation and a brief example for each word.

Words About Bugs

gathered *v.* brought things together *The ants gathered all the crumbs and carried them away.*

hill *n.* a pile of dirt *Ants, termites, and other bugs build homes that look like small hills.*

tunnel *n.* a long hole under the ground *The wasps lived in a tunnel under the ground.*

worker *n.* someone who does work *Bugs have to be hard workers to get all the food they need to live.*

Discuss Guide children to see the relationship between each word and the category. Ask children to think of sentences about bugs. Prompt them to use the words.

Read Aloud Explain that you will read aloud a story about how ants live. Then read aloud "Amazing Ants." Discuss the Comprehension questions.

Day 2

Categorize and Classify

Reread and Explain Reread "Amazing Ants." At the end of each sentence that includes an oral vocabulary word, stop and repeat the explanation of the word. Then reread the sentence.

Use a Graphic Organizer Use the graphic organizer and the questions below to reinforce understanding of the relationship between each word and the category.

```
    worker      gathered
         \    /
     Words About Work
            |
     Words About Places
          to Live
         /    \
     tunnel    hill
```

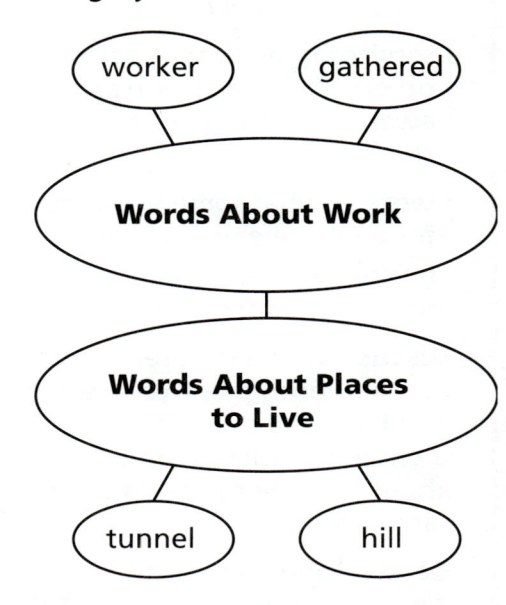

1. What are some other words for work that bugs do? What are some other words for places bugs might live? Add these words to the graphic organizer. (Sample answers: Work: drag, dig; Live: nest, hole)

2. What word might you use to describe what a gopher digs? (**tunnel**)

3. A person digs dirt to build a **tunnel**. What is that person called? (**worker**)

4. What are some things you could **gather** from an orchard? (Sample answer: apples, pumpkins)

15-20 Minute Lessons

Unit 1
Lesson 5

Day 3

Introduce Meanings

Explain Write each oral vocabulary word below on the board. Read it aloud. Offer an explanation and a brief example for each word.

Words About a Visit to the Doctor

break *n.* in more than one piece *The x-ray showed the break in the man's finger.*

healed *v.* got better after being hurt *The cut on my knee healed after a week.*

illness *n.* being sick *The girl needed medicine for her illness to get better.*

injury *n.* when the body is hurt *You could get an injury if you run inside the house.*

Discuss Guide children to see the relationship between each word and the category. Ask questions such as these: Is a **break** a kind of **injury** or **illness**? How does a break **heal**?

Read Aloud Explain that you will read aloud a story about a rabbit that must visit the doctor. Then read aloud "The Sledding Accident." Discuss the Comprehension questions.

Day 4

Categorize and Classify

Reread and Explain Reread "The Sledding Accident." At the end of each sentence that includes an oral vocabulary word, stop and repeat the explanation of the word. Then reread the sentence.

Use a Graphic Organizer Use the graphic organizer and the questions below to reinforce understanding of the relationship between each word and the category.

Not Healthy	Healthy
illness break injury	healed

1. What are some other words about being healthy? Add these to the graphic organizer. (Sample answers: strong; cured; rested)

2. What kind of **injury** might a person get from falling out of a tree? (Sample answers: a cut; a bruise; a broken bone)

3. What are some things people can do when they have an **illness**? (Sample answers: take medicine; stay in bed and rest; see the doctor)

Day 5

Deepen Understanding

Review Repeat explanations for all oral vocabulary words. Use the definitions and examples from Day 1 and Day 3.

Guide Partner Activities Have partners work together to complete each of the activities below. Circulate and listen to partners as they work. Provide corrective feedback.

Examples Describe a time when you had an **injury**. Did you ever have a **break** in a bone? Explain how you felt. Then tell about how it **healed**.

Role-Play Show a partner what kind of **worker** you want to be when you grow up.

Describe Work with a partner. Describe the things you would **gather** to bring to a picnic.

Compare Talk to your partner. Tell how you would move in a **tunnel**. Tell how you would move on a **hill**. Compare the different ways you would move.

Draw Make a get-well card for someone you know who has an **illness**. Show your card to a partner.

Assess To assess what word meanings children have learned, copy and distribute the **Pretest/Posttest** on pages 100–101. Use page 66 to administer the test. Compare scores with Day 1 assessment.

Unit 1, Lesson 5 • **T11**

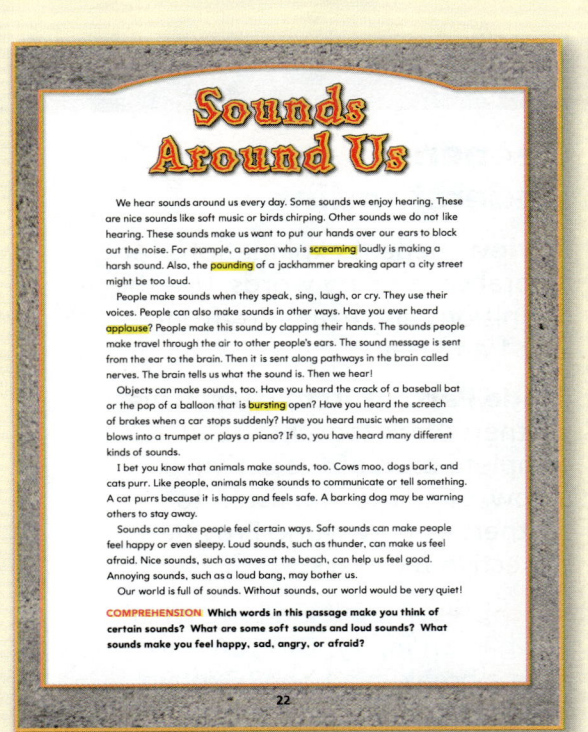

Unit 2
Lesson 6

Sounds Around Us

We hear sounds around us every day. Some sounds we enjoy hearing. These are nice sounds like soft music or birds chirping. Other sounds we do not like hearing. These sounds make us want to put our hands over our ears to block out the noise. For example, a person who is **screaming** loudly is making a harsh sound. Also, the **pounding** of a jackhammer breaking apart a city street might be too loud.

People make sounds when they speak, sing, laugh, or cry. They use their voices. People can also make sounds in other ways. Have you ever heard **applause**? People make this sound by clapping their hands. The sounds people make travel through the air to other people's ears. The sound message is sent from the ear to the brain. Then it is sent along pathways in the brain called nerves. The brain tells us what the sound is. Then we hear!

Objects can make sounds, too. Have you heard the crack of a baseball bat or the pop of a balloon that is **bursting** open? Have you heard the screech of brakes when a car stops suddenly? Have you heard music when someone blows into a trumpet or plays a piano? If so, you have heard many different kinds of sounds.

I bet you know that animals make sounds, too. Cows moo, dogs bark, and cats purr. Like people, animals make sounds to communicate or tell something. A cat purrs because it is happy and feels safe. A barking dog may be warning others to stay away.

Sounds can make people feel certain ways. Soft sounds can make people feel happy or even sleepy. Loud sounds, such as thunder, can make us feel afraid. Nice sounds, such as waves at the beach, can help us feel good. Annoying sounds, such as a loud bang, may bother us.

Our world is full of sounds. Without sounds, our world would be very quiet!

COMPREHENSION Which words in this passage make you think of certain sounds? What are some soft sounds and loud sounds? What sounds make you feel happy, sad, angry, or afraid?

22

Days 1 and 2

"Sounds Around Us," Vol. 1, pp. 22–23

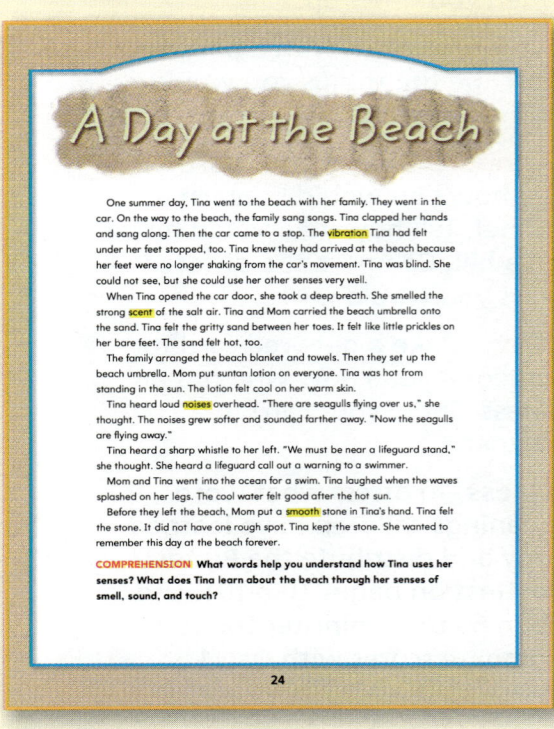

A Day at the Beach

One summer day, Tina went to the beach with her family. They went in the car. On the way to the beach, the family sang songs. Tina clapped her hands and sang along. Then the car came to a stop. The **vibration** Tina had felt under her feet stopped, too. Tina knew they had arrived at the beach because her feet were no longer shaking from the car's movement. Tina was blind. She could not see, but she could use her other senses very well.

When Tina opened the car door, she took a deep breath. She smelled the strong **scent** of the salt air. Tina and Mom carried the beach umbrella onto the sand. Tina felt the gritty sand between her toes. It felt like little prickles on her bare feet. The sand felt hot, too.

The family arranged the beach blanket and towels. Then they set up the beach umbrella. Mom put suntan lotion on everyone. Tina was hot from standing in the sun. The lotion felt cool on her warm skin.

Tina heard loud **noises** overhead. "There are seagulls flying over us," she thought. The noises grew softer and sounded farther away. "Now the seagulls are flying away."

Tina heard a sharp whistle to her left. "We must be near a lifeguard stand," she thought. She heard a lifeguard call out a warning to a swimmer.

Mom and Tina went into the ocean for a swim. Tina laughed when the waves splashed on her legs. The cool water felt good after the hot sun.

Before they left the beach, Mom put a **smooth** stone in Tina's hand. Tina felt the stone. It did not have one rough spot. Tina kept the stone. She wanted to remember this day at the beach forever.

COMPREHENSION What words help you understand how Tina uses her senses? What does Tina learn about the beach through her senses of smell, sound, and touch?

24

Days 3 and 4

"A Day at the Beach," Vol. 1, pp. 24–25

Assessment

Pretest/Posttest Administration p. 67

Pretest/Posttest Blackline Masters pp. 102–103

T12 • Curious About Words

Day 1

Introduce Meanings

Assess To assess what word meanings children already know, copy and distribute the **Pretest/Posttest** on pages 102–103. Use page 67 to administer the test.

Explain Write each oral vocabulary word below on the board. Read it aloud. Offer an explanation and a brief example for each word.

Words About Sounds

applause *n.* clapping *When we finished our play, the* applause *from our family was very loud.*

bursting *v.* popping *The fireworks were* bursting *in the sky and making lots of loud popping noises.*

pounding *n.* a hammering sound *She listened to the* pounding *of the ocean waves against the rocks.*

screaming *v.* yelling in a high, loud voice *Kayla started* screaming *so that her brother would listen to her.*

Discuss Guide children to see the relationship between each word and the category. Prompt them to tell about times when they have heard these sounds.

Read Aloud Explain that you will read aloud a story about the different kinds of sounds people hear. Then read aloud "Sounds Around Us." Discuss the Comprehension questions.

Day 2

Categorize and Classify

Reread and Explain Reread "Sounds Around Us." At the end of each sentence that includes an oral vocabulary word, stop and repeat the explanation of the word. Then reread the sentence.

Use a Graphic Organizer Use the graphic organizer and the questions below to reinforce understanding of the relationship between each word and the category.

```
         Words to Describe
         a Fireworks Show
          /      |      \
    bursting  pounding  applause
```

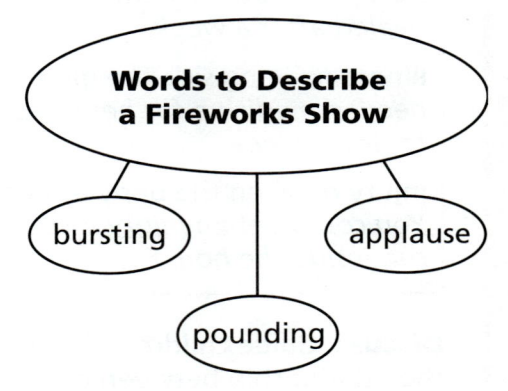

1. What could you do to make a bubble **burst**? (Sample answer: poke it with your finger)

2. What word could you use to describe the opposite of whispering? (**screaming**)

3. When might people give **applause**? (Sample answers: at plays; at concerts; at sports games)

4. What word could you use to describe the sound drums make? (**pounding**)

15-20 Minute Lessons

Unit 2

Lesson 6

Day 3

Introduce Meanings

Explain Write each oral vocabulary word below on the board. Read it aloud. Offer an explanation and a brief example for each word.

Words About Our Senses

noises *n.* things that you can hear *Farm animals make lots of different <u>noises</u>, such as moos and oinks.*

scent *n.* a smell *The <u>scent</u> of pizza filled the small restaurant.*

smooth *adj.* even; not rough *The baby's skin is soft and <u>smooth</u>.*

vibration *n.* shaking *The <u>vibration</u> of the cell phone means someone is calling.*

Discuss Guide children to see the relationship between each word and the category. Prompt them to point to things in the classroom that make **noises** or **vibrations**.

Read Aloud Explain that you will read aloud a story about how a blind girl uses her senses when she goes to the beach. Then read aloud "A Day at the Beach." Discuss the Comprehension questions.

Day 4

Categorize and Classify

Reread and Explain Reread "A Day at the Beach." At the end of each sentence that includes an oral vocabulary word, stop and repeat the explanation of the word. Then reread the sentence.

Use a Graphic Organizer Use the graphic organizer and the questions below to reinforce understanding of the relationship between each word and the category.

Words About Touch	Words About Smell	Words About Sound
smooth vibration	scent	noises

1. What **noises** do you hear when you go outside? (Sample answer: cars, lawnmowers, people talking)

2. Look around the room and find something **smooth**. Does it have a **scent**? If not, find something else that does. What does it smell like? (Answers will vary.)

3. Tell which of these things make **vibrations:** cars, birds, washing machines, flowers. (cars, washing machines)

Day 5

Deepen Understanding

Review Repeat explanations for all oral vocabulary words. Use the definitions and examples from Day 1 and Day 3.

Guide Partner Activities Have partners work together to complete each of the activities below. Circulate and listen to partners as they work. Provide corrective feedback.

Describe Talk to your partner. Tell about a time when you heard **applause**. Did you clap, too? Why or why not?

Role-Play Show a partner how you might look if you smelled the **scent** of a flower. Now show how you might look if you smelled the scent of a skunk. Finally, show how you might look if you felt the **vibrations** and heard the **pounding** of a hammer near you.

Examples Think about your toys. What are some toys that are **smooth**? Tell your partner.

Compare Talk to your partner. Describe the **noise** that a balloon makes when it **bursts**. Now describe the noise a baby makes when it is **screaming**. Compare both noises. Talk about which noise you think sounds worse.

Assess To assess what word meanings children have learned, copy and distribute the **Pretest/Posttest** on pages 102–103. Use page 67 to administer the test. Compare scores with Day 1 Assessment.

Unit 2, Lesson 6 • **T13**

Unit 2
Lesson 7

Whale Songs

Can whales sing? Some people say they can. Scientists have learned that whales can make sounds that are like singing. A whale song can last up to thirty minutes. Whales use these songs to talk to each other.

Scientists record different whale songs, or calls. Then they listen to the recordings and study the sounds. The scientists are trying to learn whether the calls mean something. Whale calls are extremely loud. The loud calls help the whales hear other whales from very far away. Some scientists believe whales are able to have conversations across long distances.

Whales use their calls to talk to each other. Some whales also use sounds to help them find things underwater. A Beluga whale, for example, makes clicking sounds and then listens for an echo. An echo happens when sound bounces off something and comes back to whatever made the sound. A Beluga whale uses this echo to find food to eat, like fish and shrimp. The echo also helps this whale stay away from objects that could be dangerous, such as the bottoms of boats. The Beluga whale knows the difference between the echo sounds, and it knows just what to do when it hears each sound.

Sounds are very important to whales. Have you ever tried to talk to a friend in a crowded room full of noises? Sometimes, sounds from people make it harder for whales to hear their own sounds. The boats that people drive create noise underwater. All this noise can make it harder for whales to talk to each other. The quieter it is in the water, the easier it is for whales to hear each other sing.

COMPREHENSION How do whales talk to each other? Which words tell about the sounds whales make?

26

Days 1 and 2

"Whale Songs," Vol. 1, pp. 26–27

The Mixed-Up Message

Mom is on her way to a meeting for work. As she runs out the door, she talks to Jim in a quiet voice. "Please tell your older brother to rake the leaves while I'm gone," she says.

Jim nods. Then he goes to find his older brother, Dennis. Jim says to Dennis, "Mom has a message for you: Take the leaves while she's gone."

"Take the leaves?" asks Dennis. "Where am I supposed to take the leaves?"

"I don't know, but it's your job now," says Jim.

"I'll ask our sister to do it," says Dennis. He finds his older sister, Karen. He says to her, "Mom has a message for you: Please take the leaves."

Karen is listening to music. "What does that mean?" she asks.

"I don't know, but it's your job now," he says.

"Bake with peas?" Karen asks. "Why would Mom want me to bake with peas?" But Dennis has already left the room.

Karen is in high school. She always does what Mom asks her to do. So Karen goes to look in the kitchen. She finds several cans of peas. She finds some butter, sugar, and flour, and she gets ready to bake. Karen thinks to herself that when Mom gets home, she will be happy that Karen did what she asked.

Karen mixes up cookie batter with peas. She bakes the cookies in the oven. Jim and Dennis come into the kitchen. Karen is taking the cookies with peas out of the oven. The whole kitchen smells like burned peas.

"What's that terrible smell?" asks Jim. Dennis wrinkles his nose.

"I'm baking with peas, just like Mom asked," Karen answers.

When Mom gets home, she smells the peas right away. "What's going on?" asks Mom.

"I got your message and did what you asked, Mom: Bake with peas," says Karen with a big smile.

Mom looks confused for a minute. She starts to giggle, and then she laughs out loud. Mom says, "What a message mix-up!"

COMPREHENSION What are some ways the family shares their thoughts and feelings? What does Mom really want her children to do? What do you think Jim will do the next time Mom gives him a message?

28

Days 3 and 4

"The Mixed-Up Message," Vol. 1, pp. 28–29

Assessment

Pretest/Posttest Administration p. 68

Pretest/Posttest Blackline Masters pp. 104–105

T14 • Curious About Words

Day 1

Introduce Meanings

Assess To assess what word meanings children already know, copy and distribute the **Pretest/Posttest** on pages 104–105. Use page 68 to administer the test.

Explain Write each oral vocabulary word below on the board. Read it aloud. Offer an explanation and a brief example for each word.

Words About Sounds

call *n.* a sound made by a person or an animal *The dog came running when it heard the call of its owner.*

hear *v.* to listen to sounds *When you hear the school bell, it is time for school to begin.*

sing *v.* to make music with your voice *The children will sing in the school concert.*

sound *n.* something that you can hear *I heard a sound coming from the other room.*

Discuss Guide children to see the relationship between each word and the category. Prompt them to use each word to talk about sounds they hear in school. Ask questions such as these: Have you ever heard a bird's **call** while playing during recess? What **sound** did the bird make?

Read Aloud Explain that you will read aloud a story about whales that use their voices to talk to one another. Then read aloud "Whale Songs." Discuss the Comprehension questions.

Day 2

Categorize and Classify

Reread and Explain Reread "Whale Songs." At the end of each sentence that includes an oral vocabulary word, stop and repeat the explanation of the word. Then reread the sentence.

Use a Graphic Organizer Use the graphic organizer and the questions below to reinforce understanding of the relationship between each word and the category.

```
        sound
          |
  Words About Making
        Sound
       /      \
    call      sing
```

1. When people **sing**, what are they doing? (making music with their voices)

2. What is a noise that you **hear** when you are outside? (Sample answers: cars; birds; the wind)

3. What are some other words about making **sound**? Add these to the graphic organizer as children suggest them. (Sample answers: chat; discuss)

15-20 Minute Lessons

Unit 2

Lesson 7

Day 3

Introduce Meanings

Explain Write each oral vocabulary word below on the board. Read it aloud. Explain that communication is what happens when people share thoughts or ideas with each other. Then offer an explanation and a brief example for each word.

Words About Communication

laughs *v.* makes a "ha ha" sound *My sister laughs at all my funny jokes.*

message *n.* the words sent from one person to another *The teacher sent a message to parents about the class party.*

talks *v.* speaks *When the school principal talks, everyone listens.*

voice *n.* the sound people make to talk *You must use a quiet voice in the library.*

Discuss Guide children to see the relationship between each word and the category. Prompt them to use the words to describe what they hear in the classroom. Point out that a message can be either spoken or written.

Read Aloud Explain that you will read aloud a story about a message that gets mixed up when a mother asks her children to do a chore. Then read aloud "The Mixed-Up Message." Discuss the Comprehension questions.

Day 4

Categorize and Classify

Reread and Explain Reread "The Mixed-Up Message." At the end of each sentence that includes an oral vocabulary word, stop and repeat the explanation of the word. Then reread the sentence.

Use a Graphic Organizer Use the graphic organizer and the questions below to reinforce understanding of the relationship between each word and the category.

Words About Things	Words About Actions
voice message	talks laughs

1. Name a place where people might **talk** in loud **voices**. (Sample answers: at a party; at a ball game)

2. You might **laugh** when you _____. (Sample answers: hear a joke; read a funny book)

3. What are some other words about actions people do to share ideas? Add these to the graphic organizer as children suggest them. (Sample answers: whisper; shout)

Day 5

Deepen Understanding

Review Repeat explanations for all oral vocabulary words. Use the definitions and examples from Day 1 and Day 3.

Guide Partner Activities Have partners work together to complete each of the activities below. Circulate and listen to partners as they work. Provide corrective feedback.

Role-Play Take turns with a partner. Name a song you can **sing**. Sing the song in a soft **voice** so only your partner can **hear** it.

Examples Think of different animals. What **sounds** do they make? Are their **calls** very different from one another? Tell your partner.

Draw Draw a picture of an imaginary animal that **talks**. Tell your partner what you would talk to this animal about.

Describe Tell your partner about a **message** you would like to give to someone in your family. Use funny words that might make the person **laugh**.

Assess To assess what word meanings children have learned, copy and distribute the **Pretest/Posttest** on pages 104–105. Use page 68 to administer the test. Compare scores with Day 1 Assessment.

Unit 2, Lesson 7 • **T15**

Unit 2
Lesson 8

Fantastic Gymnastics

Have you ever watched someone swing high on a bar or try to stand up tall on a balance beam? That person is called a gymnast, and the sport is called gymnastics. Gymnastics is a sport that takes a lot of hard work.

There are different kinds of gymnastics. Two very common kinds are artistic gymnastics and rhythmic gymnastics. Both men and women compete in artistic gymnastics, but only women compete in rhythmic gymnastics.

Artistic gymnasts do their routines on special equipment. Balance beams, parallel bars, uneven parallel bars, and rings are all examples of this equipment. Artistic gymnasts also do floor exercises. During floor exercises, gymnasts leap and spin. They may stop at times, as if they're taking a rest. But then they'll run across the floor and do an exciting flip!

Rhythmic gymnasts combine gymnastics with dance. They do their exercises with music playing in the background, like dancers do. Rhythmic gymnasts use equipment such as balls, hoops, and ribbons. A rhythmic gymnast may twirl the ribbon in a circular motion. The twirling matches the music. Rhythmic gymnasts bend their bodies in ways that other people cannot bend. They can make their bodies into shapes. It is very beautiful to watch.

Gymnasts are so amazing to watch because they are very strong. They are also very good at focusing. Some artistic gymnasts must use their arm and leg muscles to swing their bodies onto high bars. Others must use their balance to do jumps and spins on a beam that is not even one foot wide—even smaller than the size of a ruler!

To become a gymnast, you need to practice a lot. Many professional gymnasts started practicing when they were as young as three years old! This practice will help to make you strong and keep you focused. The more you practice, the better gymnast you will be!

One great thing about gymnastics is that anyone can try it. If you think you would have fun leaping and doing flips, gymnastics might be the sport for you!

COMPREHENSION Which words tell about movement in gymnastics? Why do gymnasts have to be strong?

30

Days 1 and 2

"Fantastic Gymnastics," Vol. 1, pp. 30–31

Animal Games

Deer lived in the forest. Each day, he walked and skipped and munched on nuts. But something was missing. Deer spent every day all by himself. He felt lonely. Deer wanted a friend to play with.

One morning, Deer heard leaves rustling in front of him. Suddenly Chipmunk burst through the pile of leaves, with Squirrel running right behind. Chipmunk and Squirrel stopped when they saw Deer.

"What are you doing?" asked Deer.

Chipmunk explained that they were playing a game called chase. One animal would run and the other animal would race after him and try to catch him.

"Ooh, that sounds like fun!" said Deer.

"It is fun," Squirrel said. "Would you like to play?"

Deer nodded his head and joined in a game of chase with Chipmunk and Squirrel. Deer liked running through the forest, chasing the other animals. His four feet pounded the ground as he tried to catch them.

The three animals quickly became good friends. They played other games, too. Chipmunk taught Deer how to play hide-and-seek. When Chipmunk hid, she curled up in a ball, her head touching her tail. It was very hard to find her. Then Chipmunk got up and sneaked behind Deer. She was so quiet, Deer didn't hear her. Chipmunk ran to the goal. She was safe.

Squirrel taught Deer how to play tag. Deer liked running in this game, too. He was very good at escaping from Squirrel. Deer would always run away before Squirrel could tag him.

Then Deer taught Chipmunk and Squirrel a new game. It was called follow-the-leader. Deer would walk and skip and munch on nuts. Chipmunk and Squirrel had to do everything that Deer did.

Deer was happy. Now he had two new friends to play with!

COMPREHENSION How do the animals move as they play the games? Why is Deer happy after he meets Chipmunk and Squirrel?

32

Days 3 and 4

"Animal Games," Vol. 1, pp. 32–33

Assessment

Pretest/Posttest Administration p. 69

Pretest/Posttest Blackline Masters pp. 106–107

T16 • Curious About Words

Day 1

Introduce Meanings

Assess To assess what word meanings children already know, copy and distribute the **Pretest/Posttest** on pages 106–107. Use page 69 to administer the test.

Explain Write each oral vocabulary word below on the board. Read it aloud. Offer an explanation and a brief example for each word.

Words About Moving Your Body

bend *v.* to make a curve *In a strong wind, trees bend to the ground.*

motion *n.* a movement *The police officer uses a hand motion to tell cars that they can go.*

muscles *n.* the parts inside your body that help you move *The girl is a good swimmer because she has strong leg muscles.*

rest *n.* when you stop moving for a while *After running around all day, I needed to take a rest.*

Discuss Guide children to see the relationship between each word and the category. Ask them to point to some of their **muscles**, and then have them demonstrate the other words.

Read Aloud Explain that you will read aloud a story about the sport of gymnastics. Then read aloud "Fantastic Gymnastics." Discuss the Comprehension questions.

Day 2

Categorize and Classify

Reread and Explain Reread "Fantastic Gymnastics." At the end of each sentence that includes an oral vocabulary word, stop and repeat the explanation of the word. Then reread the sentence.

Use a Graphic Organizer Use the graphic organizer and the questions below to reinforce understanding of the relationship between each word and the category.

Words About Moving	Words About Not Moving
bend motion	rest

1. What is a way people can use their leg **muscles**? (Sample answers: walk; run; jump)

2. What are some other words you can use to talk about not moving? Add these to the graphic organizer as children suggest them. (Sample answers: stop; pause; freeze)

3. When you wave to a friend, you are making a _____. (motion)

15-20 Minute Lessons

Unit 2

Lesson 8

Day 3

Introduce Meanings

Explain Write each oral vocabulary word below on the board. Read it aloud. Offer an explanation and a brief example for each word.

Words About Animal Actions

curled *v.* twisted into a curved shape *The cat curled itself on the bed for a nap.*

escaping *v.* getting away *The horse keeps escaping from the field by jumping over the fence.*

race *v.* to run fast *We saw a fox race across the field.*

sneaked *v.* did something in a secret way *The cat sneaked some food off the kitchen table.*

Discuss Guide children to see the relationship between each word and the category. Prompt them to use each word to describe how an animal moves.

Read Aloud Explain that you will read aloud a story about animal friends that play together. Then read aloud "Animal Games." Discuss the Comprehension questions.

Day 4

Categorize and Classify

Reread and Explain Reread "Animal Games." At the end of each sentence that includes an oral vocabulary word, stop and repeat the explanation of the word. Then reread the sentence.

Use a Graphic Organizer Use the graphic organizer and the questions below to reinforce understanding of the relationship between each word and the category.

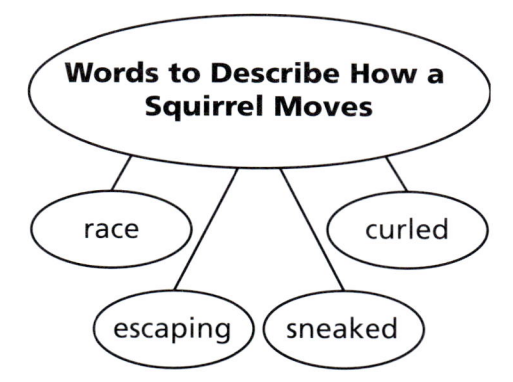

Words to Describe How a Squirrel Moves
- race
- curled
- escaping
- sneaked

1. Imagine a squirrel was **racing** away from a dog that was chasing it. What word might describe that? **(escaping)**

2. If a squirrel **curled** its tail, would the tail be sticking straight out or curved up? **(curved up)**

3. A squirrel **sneaked** into a house through an open window. Does the squirrel belong in the house? **(no)**

Day 5

Deepen Understanding

Review Repeat explanations for all oral vocabulary words. Use the definitions and examples from Day 1 and Day 3.

Guide Partner Activities Have partners work together to complete each of the activities below. Circulate and listen to partners as they work. Provide corrective feedback.

Compare Talk to your partner. Compare how someone runs to how someone moves in gymnastics. Use these words: **race, bend.** Show the different **motions** people use for each one.

Examples Talk to your partner. Tell about a time you **sneaked** somewhere. Explain what happened.

Describe Talk to your partner. Tell how a rabbit might **escape** from a fox.

Role-Play Show how your fingers look when you **curl** them. What else can you curl?

Draw Draw a picture showing how you use your **muscles**. Then draw a picture showing how you stop for a **rest**. Share your pictures with your partner.

Assess To assess what word meanings children have learned, copy and distribute the **Pretest/Posttest** on pages 106–107. Use page 69 to administer the test. Compare scores with Day 1 Assessment.

Unit 2, Lesson 8 • **T17**

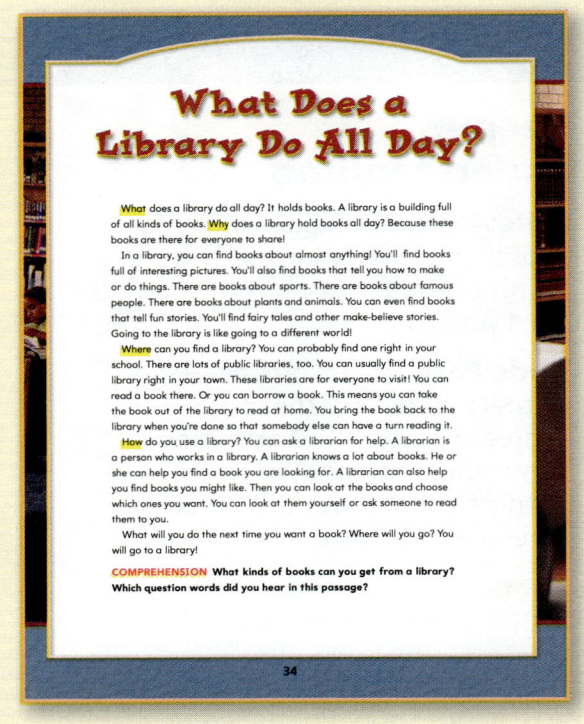

Unit 2
Lesson 9

Days 1 and 2
"What Does a Library Do All Day?" Vol. 1, pp. 34–35

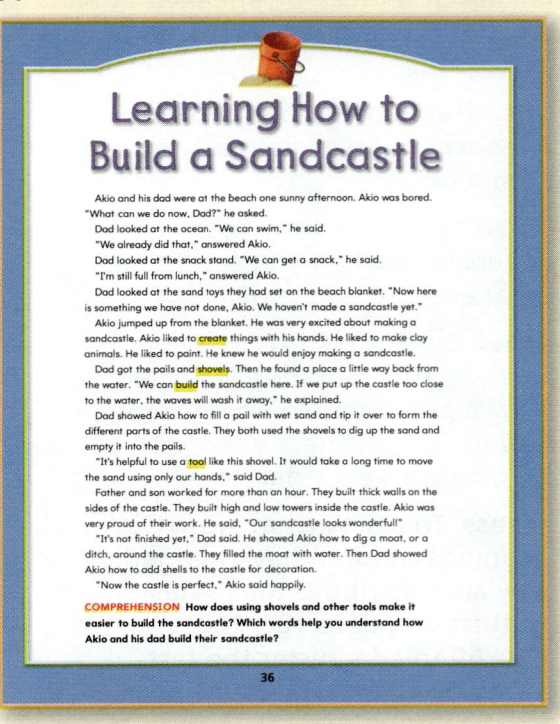

Days 3 and 4
"Learning How to Build a Sandcastle," Vol. 1, pp. 36–37

Assessment
Pretest/Posttest Administration p. 70

Pretest/Posttest Blackline Masters pp. 108–109

T18 • Curious About Words

Day 1

Introduce Meanings

Assess To assess what word meanings children already know, copy and distribute the **Pretest/Posttest** on pages 108–109. Use page 70 to administer the test.

Explain Write each oral vocabulary word below on the board. Read it aloud. Offer an explanation and a brief example for each word.

Words About Asking Questions

how *adv.* used to ask a question about the way something is done *How do you make pizza?*

what *pron.* used to ask a question about people or things *What is your friend's name?*

where *adv.* used to ask a question about the place of something *Where is the bike?*

why *adv.* used to ask a question about what makes something happen *Why is it dark at night?*

Discuss Guide children to see the relationship between each word and the category. Have partners ask each other questions using the words.

Read Aloud Explain that you will read aloud a story about the library. Then read aloud "What Does a Library Do All Day?" Discuss the Comprehension questions.

Day 2

Categorize and Classify

Reread and Explain Reread "What Does a Library Do All Day?" At the end of each sentence that includes an oral vocabulary word, stop and repeat the explanation of the word. Then reread the sentence.

Use a Graphic Organizer Use the graphic organizer and the questions below to reinforce understanding of the relationship between each word and the category.

Question Words: how, why, what, where

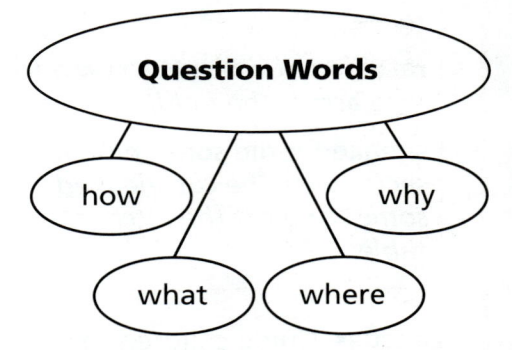

1. **What** has leaves? (Sample answers: a tree; a bush; a flower)
2. **Where** might you see a tree? (Sample answers: in a park; in the woods; in a yard)
3. **How** do you plant a tree? (Sample answer: You put a seed in the ground.)
4. Do you like trees? **Why** do you like them or why don't you like them? (Answers will vary.)

15-20 Minute Lessons

Unit 2

Lesson 9

Day 3

Introduce Meanings

Explain Write each oral vocabulary word below on the board. Read it aloud. Offer an explanation and a brief example for each word.

Words About Building Things
build *v.* to put together *The children will build a birdhouse out of wood.* **create** *v.* to make *In art class, we will create colorful paintings.* **shovels** *n.* tools used for digging *The family used shovels to dig a hole for the new tree they were planting.* **tool** *n.* a thing that people use to help them do work *A rake is a good tool for cleaning up leaves.*

Discuss Guide children to see the relationship between each word and the category. Ask questions such as these: What would you like to **build**? Did you **create** anything last week? Have you ever used a **shovel** or another **tool**?

Read Aloud Explain that you will read aloud a story about a boy and his father who work together to build a sandcastle. Then read aloud "Learning How to Build a Sandcastle." Discuss the Comprehension questions.

Day 4

Categorize and Classify

Reread and Explain Reread "Learning How to Build a Sandcastle." At the end of each sentence that includes an oral vocabulary word, stop and repeat the explanation of the word. Then reread the sentence.

Use a Graphic Organizer Use the graphic organizer and the questions below to reinforce understanding of the relationship between each word and the category.

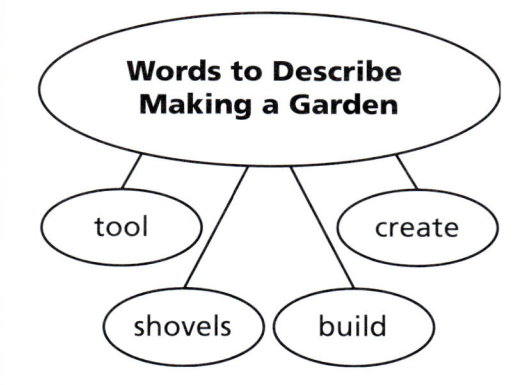

```
        Words to Describe
        Making a Garden
         /    |    |    \
      tool         create
       shovels   build
```

1. A family needs to dig holes in the ground to make a garden. What **tool** will they use? (a **shovel**)

2. Why might the family **build** a fence around their garden? (Sample answer: to keep animals from eating the plants)

3. What could the family use to **create** a sign for their garden? (Sample answer: paper, markers)

Day 5

Deepen Understanding

Review Repeat explanations for all oral vocabulary words. Use the definitions and examples from Day 1 and Day 3.

Guide Partner Activities Have partners work together to complete each of the activities below. Circulate and listen to partners as they work. Provide corrective feedback.

Categorize Talk to your partner. What are three games you like to play? Where can you play these games? Now tell which game is your favorite.

Examples What are some things you can **create** in art class? Tell your partner.

Describe Tell your partner about a food you really like to eat. Why do you like it so much?

Role-Play Pretend you are a carpenter. What will you **build**? What **tools** will you use? Show your partner.

Draw Imagine your dog buried one of your toys. How could you use a **shovel** to dig it up? Draw a picture to show how you would do it.

Assess To assess what word meanings children have learned, copy and distribute the **Pretest/Posttest** on pages 108–109. Use page 70 to administer the test. Compare scores with Day 1 Assessment.

Unit 2, Lesson 9 • **T19**

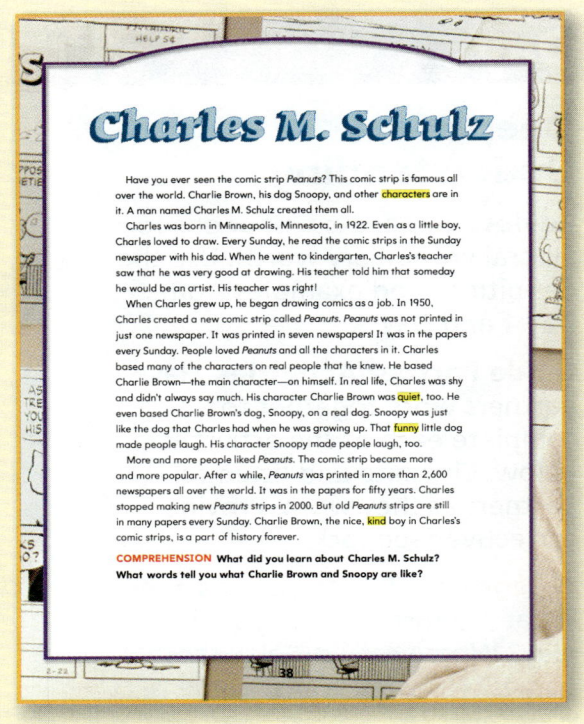

Unit 2
Lesson 10

Days 1 and 2

"Charles M. Schulz," Vol. 1, pp. 38–39

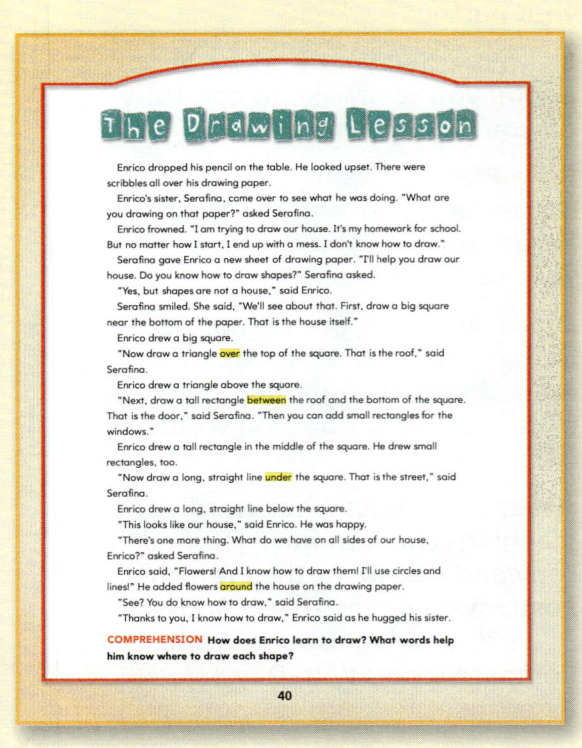

Days 3 and 4

"The Drawing Lesson," Vol. 1, pp. 40–41

Assessment

Pretest/Posttest Administration p. 71

Pretest/Posttest Blackline Masters pp. 110–111

T20 • Curious About Words

Day 1

Introduce Meanings

Assess To assess what word meanings children already know, copy and distribute the **Pretest/Posttest** on pages 110–111. Use page 71 to administer the test.

Explain Write each oral vocabulary word below on the board. Read it aloud. Offer an explanation and a brief example for each word.

Words About What People Are Like
character *n.* a person in a book or a show *Goldilocks is a character in a book.*
funny *adj.* making people laugh *My brother told a funny joke.*
kind *adj.* nice; helpful *Our kind neighbor took care of our cat when we went on vacation.*
quiet *adj.* making very little noise *The children were quiet as they listened to the teacher read the story.*

Discuss Guide children to see the relationship between each word and the category. Ask questions such as these: *What words would you use to talk about a friend? What words would you use to talk about someone in a book?*

Read Aloud Explain that you will read aloud a story about a man who created a famous cartoon. Then read aloud "Charles M. Schulz." Discuss the Comprehension questions.

Day 2

Categorize and Classify

Reread and Explain Reread "Charles M. Schulz." At the end of each sentence that includes an oral vocabulary word, stop and repeat the explanation of the word. Then reread the sentence.

Use a Graphic Organizer Use the graphic organizer and the questions below to reinforce understanding of the relationship between each word and the category.

Words About a Friend
- kind
- funny
- quiet

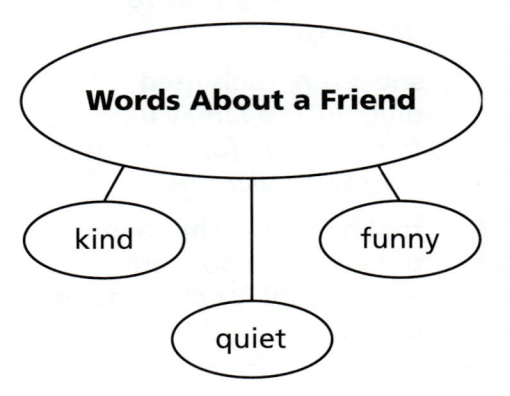

1. A good friend is **kind.** What are some other words that tell what a good friend is like? Add these to the graphic organizer as children suggest them. (Sample answers: nice; polite; helpful)

2. Name a **character** from a book. (Sample answers: Frog; Toad; Curious George)

3. Someone who doesn't talk a lot is _____. (**quiet**)

15-20 Minute Lessons

Unit 2

Lesson 10

Day 3

Introduce Meanings

Explain Write each oral vocabulary word below on the board. Read it aloud. Offer an explanation and a brief example for each word.

Words That Tell Where

around *prep.* on all sides of *Our teacher told us to sit in a circle around her.*

between *prep.* in the middle of *I am sitting between my friend Carlos and my friend Molly.*

over *prep.* above *Workers built a bridge over a river.*

under *prep.* below *Boats on the river pass under the bridge.*

Discuss Guide children to see the relationship between each word and the category. Point to different objects in the classroom and prompt children to use the words to tell where the objects are.

Read Aloud Explain that you will read aloud a story about a girl who helps her brother learn to draw. Then read aloud "The Drawing Lesson." Discuss the Comprehension questions.

Day 4

Categorize and Classify

Reread and Explain Reread "The Drawing Lesson." At the end of each sentence that includes an oral vocabulary word, stop and repeat the explanation of the word. Then reread the sentence.

Use a Graphic Organizer Use the graphic organizer and the questions below to reinforce understanding of the relationship between each word and the category.

```
      Words That Help You
          Find Things
       /      |    \
     over         between
     under       around
```

1. Name two things you might find **under** your bed. (Sample answer: a toy car, a doll)
2. What is something that might hang **over** your bed? (Sample answer: a poster)
3. If you were cold at night, what would you put **around** you in bed? (Sample answer: a blanket)

Day 5

Deepen Understanding

Review Repeat explanations for all oral vocabulary words. Use the definitions and examples from Day 1 and Day 3.

Guide Partner Activities Have partners work together to complete each of the activities below. Circulate and listen to partners as they work. Provide corrective feedback.

Discuss Talk to your partner. Tell about **characters** from stories you know that are **kind**. Then tell about characters that are not kind. What do you like about these characters? What don't you like about them?

Role-Play Now pretend to be one of these characters. Act out what the character does and says. Is the character **quiet** or does he or she talk a lot?

Describe Talk to your partner. Tell about something you see on your trip **between** home and school.

Examples Tell your partner about something that is **funny**. Try to tell it in a way that makes your partner laugh.

Draw Look at what is **over** your head. Look at what is **under** your feet. Draw what you see all **around** you in the classroom. Look at your partner's picture and talk about what you each drew.

Assess To assess what word meanings children have learned, copy and distribute the **Pretest/Posttest** on pages 110–111. Use page 71 to administer the test. Compare scores with Day 1 assessment.

Unit 2, Lesson 10 • **T21**

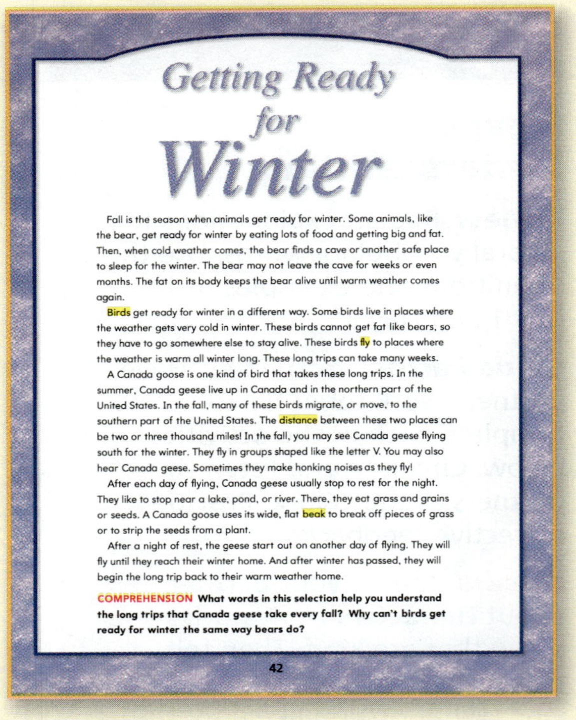

Unit 3
Lesson 11

Days 1 and 2
"Getting Ready for Winter," Vol. 1, pp. 42–43

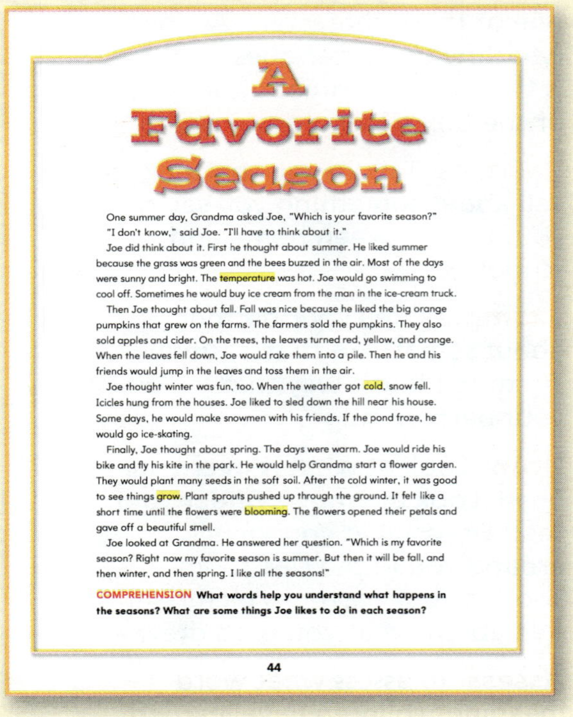

Days 3 and 4
"A Favorite Season," Vol. 1, pp. 44–45

Assessment
Pretest/Posttest Administration p. 72

Pretest/Posttest Blackline Masters pp. 112–113

T22 • Curious About Words

Day 1

Introduce Meanings

Assess To assess what word meanings children already know, copy and distribute the **Pretest/Posttest** on pages 112–113. Use page 72 to administer the test.

Explain Write each oral vocabulary word below on the board. Read it aloud. Explain that migration is when birds travel from one place to another. Then offer an explanation and a brief example for each word.

Words About Migration

beaks *n.* the hard parts of birds' mouths *Mother birds use their beaks to feed their babies worms.*

bird *n.* an animal with wings and feathers *A duck is one kind of bird that quacks and swims.*

distance *n.* the amount of space between two places *The distance between the two towns is one hundred miles.*

fly *v.* to move through the air *Some ducks fly south when the weather gets cold.*

Discuss Guide children to see the relationship between each word and the category. Ask questions such as these: What kinds of **birds** do you see during the summer? What kinds of birds do you see during the winter? How do birds get from one place to another?

Read Aloud Explain that you will read aloud a story about how animals get ready for winter. Then read aloud "Getting Ready for Winter." Discuss the Comprehension questions.

Day 2

Categorize and Classify

Reread and Explain Reread "Getting Ready for Winter." At the end of each sentence that includes an oral vocabulary word, stop and repeat the explanation of the word. Then reread the sentence.

Use a Graphic Organizer Use the graphic organizer and the questions below to reinforce understanding of the relationship between each word and the category.

Words About Traveling
- fly
- distance

Words About Birds
- beaks

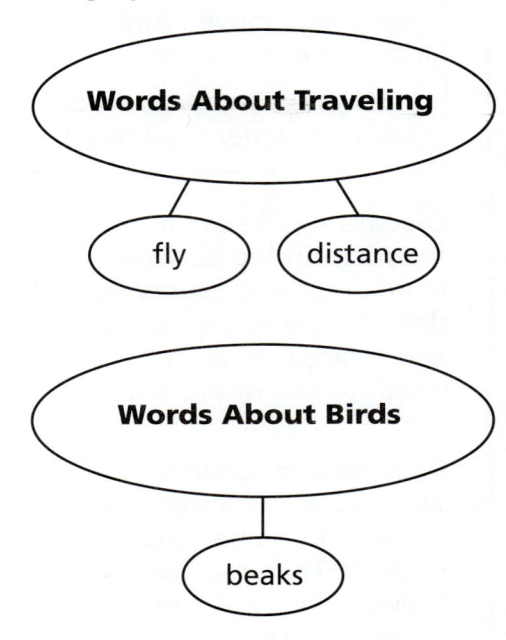

1. What might you look at to find the **distance** between two places? (Sample answer: a map)

2. Name some things that **birds** do. (Sample answer: **fly**, sing, eat, build nests, lay eggs)

3. Where do you find the **beak** on a bird? What are some other parts of a bird's body? Add these to the second graphic organizer as children suggest them. (Sample answers: mouth; wing; tail; head)

15-20 Minute Lessons

Unit 3

Lesson 11

Day 3

Introduce Meanings

Explain Write each oral vocabulary word below on the board. Offer an explanation and a brief example for each word.

Words About Seasons

blooming *v.* making flowers *We can pick roses when the rosebush is <u>blooming</u>.*

cold *adj.* chilly *I wear a heavy coat when the weather is <u>cold</u>.*

grow *v.* to get bigger *In the summer, we water our garden to help the plants <u>grow</u>.*

temperature *n.* how hot or cold it is *If the <u>temperature</u> is hot, you might want to have a cool drink.*

Discuss Guide children to see the relationship between each word and the category. Prompt them to use words to talk about their favorite season. Guide them to talk about what happens in nature during their favorite season.

Read Aloud Explain that you will read aloud a story about a boy who tries to decide which season he likes best. Then read aloud "A Favorite Season." Discuss the Comprehension questions.

Day 4

Categorize and Classify

Reread and Explain Reread "A Favorite Season." At the end of each sentence that includes an oral vocabulary word, stop and repeat the explanation of the word. Then reread the sentence.

Use a Graphic Organizer Use the graphic organizer and the questions below to reinforce understanding of the relationship between each word and the category.

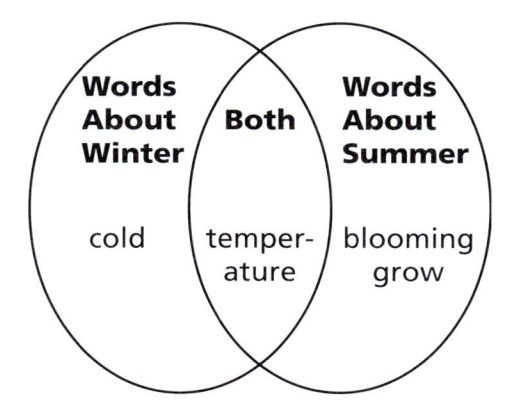

Words About Winter: cold
Both: temperature
Words About Summer: blooming, grow

1. What are some more words about winter? What are some more words about summer? Add these to the graphic organizer as children suggest them. (Sample answers: snow; ice; hot, swimming)

2. Why is **temperature** in both Words About Winter and Words About Summer? (Sample answer: because temperature can be hot or cold)

3. Name something that is **cold**. (Sample answers: ice cream; snow; ice)

4. Suppose you saw flowers **growing** on a plant. What word might describe that? (**blooming**)

Day 5

Deepen Understanding

Review Repeat explanations for all oral vocabulary words. Use the definitions and examples from Day 1 and Day 3.

Guide Partner Activities Have partners work together to complete each of the activities below. Circulate and listen to partners as they work. Provide corrective feedback.

Describe Tell about a time when you traveled a long **distance**. Where did you go? How did you get there? Tell your partner.

Examples What are some things you might see **blooming**? Tell your partner.

Role-Play Pretend you are planting a bean seed. Show your partner what you would do to help the bean plant **grow**.

Draw Draw a picture of a **bird**. Show how the bird uses its wings to **fly**. Draw its **beak**, wings, and feet.

Discuss Talk to your partner about how you can stay warm when the **temperature** is **cold**. Then talk about how you can stay cool when the temperature is hot.

Assess To assess what word meanings children have learned, copy and distribute the **Pretest/Posttest** on pages 112–113. Use page 72 to administer the test. Compare scores with Day 1 assessment.

Unit 3, Lesson 11 • **T23**

Unit 3
Lesson 12

Days 1 and 2

"Tornadoes," Vol. 1, pp. 46–47

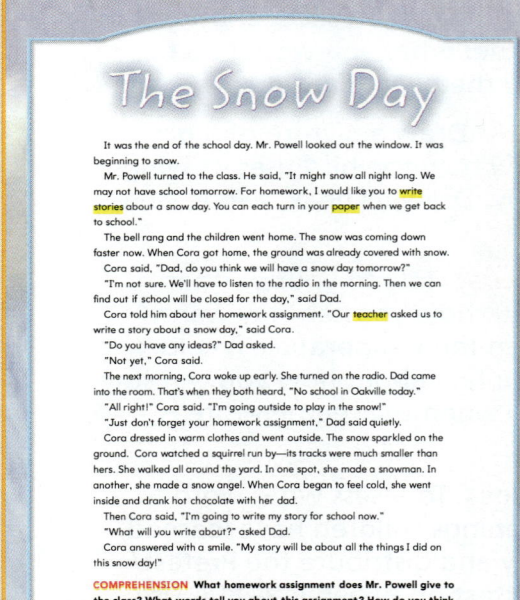

Days 3 and 4

"The Snow Day," Vol. 1, pp. 48–49

Assessment

Pretest/Posttest Administration p. 73

Pretest/Posttest Blackline Masters pp. 114–115

T24 • Curious About Words

Day 1

Introduce Meanings

Explain To assess what word meanings children already know, copy and distribute the **Pretest/Posttest** on pages T114–T115. Use page 73 to administer the test.

Explain Write each oral vocabulary word below on the board. Read it aloud. Offer an explanation and a brief example for each word.

Words About Storms

damage *v.* to harm or break *I'm worried that the heavy snow will damage our roof.*

dangerous *adj.* likely to hurt people or things *Keep safe by staying inside during dangerous lightning storms.*

shake *v.* to move something side to side or up and down very quickly *The winds were strong enough to shake the whole house.*

wind *n.* air that moves *The wind began to blow so hard, it lifted the trash can off the ground.*

Discuss Guide children to see the relationship between each word and the category. Ask questions such as these: When have you felt strong **winds**? In what ways can a strong wind be **dangerous**?

Read Aloud Explain that you will read aloud a story about a type of storm called a tornado. Then read aloud "Tornadoes." Discuss the Comprehension questions.

Day 2

Categorize and Classify

Reread and Explain Reread "Tornadoes." At the end of each sentence that includes an oral vocabulary word, stop and repeat the explanation of the word. Then reread the sentence.

Use a Graphic Organizer Use the graphic organizer and the questions below to reinforce understanding of the relationship between each word and the category.

[Graphic organizer: Words About Dangerous Storms — shake, wind, dangerous, damage]

1. What can a storm do to **damage** things? (Sample answer: It can have strong winds that knock things over.)

2. Name three things in a house that might **shake** in a strong **wind**. (Sample answer: walls, doors, windows)

3. A tornado is one kind of **dangerous** storm. What other kinds of dangerous storms can you name? (Sample answer: hurricane, thunderstorm, blizzard)

15-20 Minute Lessons

Unit 3

Lesson 12

Day 3

Introduce Meanings

Explain Write each oral vocabulary word below on the board. Read it aloud. Offer an explanation and a brief example for each word.

Words About School

paper *n.* schoolwork *The teacher asked us to write a paper about dinosaurs.*

stories *n.* things that tell what happened; what happened might be real or made-up *This book has stories about animals.*

teacher *n.* a person who gives lessons *The teacher showed the children how to add numbers.*

write *v.* to think up and put in words *I will write a fairy tale.*

Discuss Guide children to see the relationship between each word and the category. Ask questions such as these: How does your **teacher** help you learn? If you could choose anything in the world to **write** about, what would it be?

Read Aloud Explain that you will read aloud a story about what happens when school is canceled because of snow. Then read aloud "The Snow Day." Discuss the Comprehension questions.

Day 4

Categorize and Classify

Read and Explain Reread "The Snow Day." At the end of each sentence that includes an oral vocabulary word, stop and repeat the explanation of the word. Then reread the sentence.

Use a Graphic Organizer Use the graphic organizer and the questions below to reinforce understanding of the relationship between each word and the category.

Words About Who We See at School	Words About What We Do at School
teacher	paper stories write

1. A **teacher** is one person you see at school. Who are some other people you see at school? Add these words to the graphic organizer as children suggest them. (Sample answers: students; principal; janitor)

2. Reading **stories** is one thing you do at school. What else do you do at school? Add these words to the graphic organizer as children suggest them. (Sample answers: draw; count; play)

Day 5

Deepen Understanding

Review Repeat explanations for all oral vocabulary words. Use the definitions and examples from Day 1 and Day 3.

Guide Partner Activities Have partners work together to complete each of the activities below. Circulate and listen to partners as they work. Provide corrective feedback.

Discuss Name some **stories** you like. Do any of them tell about **dangerous** animals? Tell your partner.

Role-Play Pretend you are a **teacher**. Pretend your partner is a student, and assign him or her a **paper**. Describe what he or she should **write** about.

Describe Talk to your partner. Describe how a strong **wind** can **damage** a tree.

Draw Think of something you have to **shake**. It could be something you eat or drink, or it could be a toy. Draw a picture of it.

Assess To assess what word meanings children have learned, copy and distribute the **Pretest/Posttest** on pages 114–115. Use page 73 to administer the test. Compare scores with Day 1 assessment.

Unit 3, Lesson 12 • **T25**

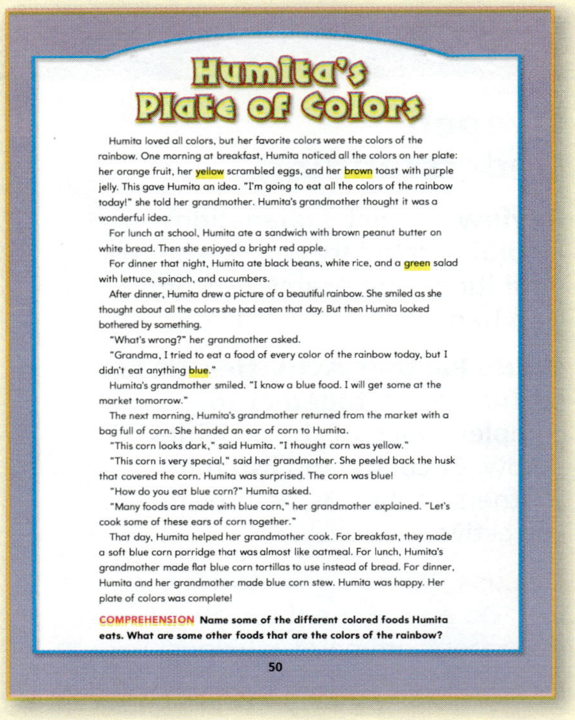

Unit 3

Lesson 13

Days 1 and 2

"Humita's Plate of Colors," Vol. 1, pp. 50–51

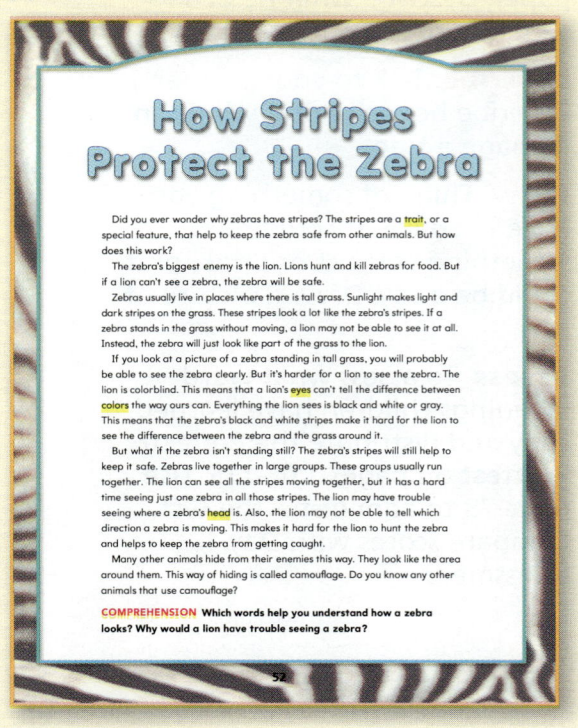

Days 3 and 4

"How Stripes Protect the Zebra," Vol. 1, pp. 52–53

Assessment

Pretest/Posttest Administration p. 74

Pretest/Posttest Blackline Masters pp. 116–117

T26 • Curious About Words

Day 1

Introduce Meanings

Assess To assess what word meanings children already know, copy and distribute the **Pretest/Posttest** on pages 116–117. Use page 74 to administer the test.

Explain Write each oral vocabulary word below on the board. Read it aloud. Offer an explanation and a brief example for each word.

Words About Colors

blue *adj.* the color of the sky *The water in the pool looks blue.*

brown *adj.* the color of chocolate *When you toast bread, it turns brown.*

green *adj.* the color of grass *In summer, the leaves on the trees are green.*

yellow *adj.* the color of the sun *Here is a bunch of yellow bananas.*

Discuss Guide children to see the relationship between each word and the category. Prompt children to use each word to talk about colors in the classroom.

Read Aloud Explain that you will read aloud a story about a girl who wants to eat foods that are all the colors of the rainbow. Then read aloud "Humita's Plate of Colors." Discuss the Comprehension questions.

Day 2

Categorize and Classify

Reread and Explain Reread "Humita's Plate of Colors." At the end of each sentence that includes an oral vocabulary word, stop and repeat the explanation of the word. Then reread the sentence.

Use a Graphic Organizer Use the graphic organizer and the questions below to reinforce understanding of the relationship between each word and the category.

Words to Describe Food: blue, yellow, green, brown

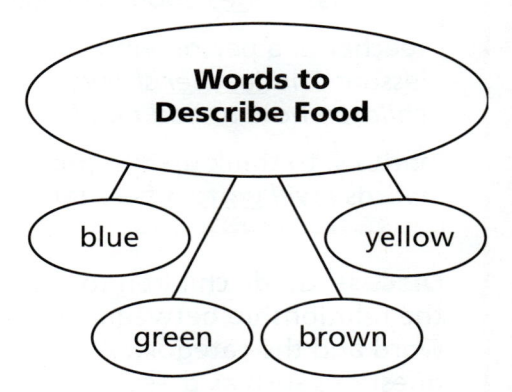

1. Name some foods that are **green**. (Sample answers: green beans, broccoli)
2. What word might you use to describe butter? (**yellow**)
3. A blueberry is a fruit that is _____. (**blue**)
4. Chocolate pudding is _____. (**brown**)

15-20 Minute Lessons

**Unit 3
Lesson 13**

Day 3

Introduce Meanings

Explain Write each oral vocabulary word below on the board. Read it aloud. Offer an explanation and a brief example for each word.

Words for Describing Animals

color *n.* how something looks on the surface *The color of the fish is yellow.*

eyes *n.* parts of the body used for seeing *The dog's eyes followed the rabbit's every move.*

head *n.* the top part of the body *An elephant has a very large head.*

trait *n.* a feature of an animal *Shiny black fur is a trait of all gorillas.*

Discuss Guide children to see the relationship between each word and the category. Display a picture of two or three animals. Prompt children to use the words to describe each animal.

Read Aloud Explain that you will read aloud a story about zebra stripes. Then read aloud "How Stripes Protect the Zebra." Discuss the Comprehension questions.

Day 4

Categorize and Classify

Reread and Explain Reread "How Stripes Protect the Zebra." At the end of each sentence that includes an oral vocabulary word, stop and repeat the explanation of the word. Then reread the sentence.

Use a Graphic Organizer Use the graphic organizer and the questions below to reinforce understanding of the relationship between each word and the category.

Words About Body Parts	Words About What Animals Are Like
eyes head	trait color

1. Where do you find the **eyes** on an animal? (Sample answer: on its **head**)

2. What are some other parts of an animal's body? Add these to the graphic organizer as children suggest them. (Sample answers: mouth; legs; tail)

3. All leopards have spotty coats. This means they share the same _____. (**trait**)

4. An animal whose **color** is gray might be _____. (Sample answers: a mouse; an elephant)

Day 5

Deepen Understanding

Review Repeat explanations for all oral vocabulary words. Use the definitions and examples from Day 1 and Day 3.

Guide Partner Activities Have partners work together to complete each of the activities below. Circulate and listen to partners as they work. Provide corrective feedback.

Examples What are some things that are **yellow**? What are some things that are **blue**? **green**? Tell your partner.

Compare Talk to your partner. Compare the **color** of the sky on a sunny day to the color of the sky when it is about to rain. Use as many color words as you can.

Describe Talk to your partner. Tell about a **trait** you have that someone related to you also has, such as eye color, hair color, or freckles.

Draw Draw a picture of someone who has **brown** hair on his or her **head**. Tell your partner who this person is.

Discuss Tell your partner about two things you can learn by using your **eyes**. Then tell about two things you can learn by using your ears.

Assess To assess what word meanings children have learned, copy and distribute the **Pretest/Posttest** on pages 116–117. Use page 74 to administer the test. Compare scores with Day 1 assessment.

Unit 3, Lesson 13 • **T27**

Unit 3

Lesson 14

Days 1 and 2

"Amazing Penguins," Vol. 1, pp. 54–55

Days 3 and 4

"A New Home for Marvin Mouse," Vol. 1, pp. 56–57

Assessment

Pretest/Posttest Administration p. 75

Pretest/Posttest Blackline Masters pp. 118–119

T28 • Curious About Words

Day 1

Introduce Meanings

Assess To assess what word meanings children already know, copy and distribute the **Pretest/Posttest** on pages 118–119. Use page 75 to administer the test.

Explain Write each oral vocabulary word below on the board. Read it aloud. Offer an explanation and a brief example for each word.

Words About Distance

area *n.* a space *Our playground has an area just for swings.*

deepest *adj.* farthest down *The man fishes in the deepest part of the river.*

far *adv.* not very close *The deer ran far away into the forest.*

near *adj.* close to *That table is near the window.*

Discuss Guide children to see the relationship between each word and the category. Ask questions and prompts such as these: Who can show me an **area** of our classroom? Is it **near** my desk or **far** from it? Now tell which is **deepest**: a puddle, a stream, or an ocean.

Read Aloud Explain that you will read aloud a story about how penguins travel to raise a family. Then read aloud "Amazing Penguins." Discuss the Comprehension questions.

Day 2

Categorize and Classify

Reread and Explain Reread "Amazing Penguins." At the end of each sentence that includes an oral vocabulary word, stop and repeat the explanation of the word. Then reread the sentence.

Use a Graphic Organizer Use the graphic organizer and the questions below to reinforce understanding of the relationship between each word and the category.

Words to Describe Hide-and-Seek
- far
- area
- near

1. If the seeker comes **near** the **area** where you are hiding, you must be _____. (Sample answer: quiet)

2. If the seeker is **far** away, you can _____. (Sample answer: run to home base)

3. It wouldn't be safe to hide in the **deepest** hole you could find. Where is a safe place to hide? (Sample answer: behind a curtain)

Unit 3
Lesson 14

15-20 Minute Lessons

Day 3

Introduce Meanings

Explain Write each oral vocabulary word below on the board. Read it aloud. Offer an explanation and a brief example for each word.

Words About Actions

climbing *v.* moving to the top *The girl is climbing the ladder on the slide.*

eat *v.* to take in food *We eat eggs and toast for breakfast.*

landing *v.* coming down to the ground after falling *The cat was landing on the table when I found him.*

live *v.* to have a home *The bears live in a cave.*

Discuss Guide children to see the relationship between each word and the category. Ask children to describe where they **live**. Then prompt them to act out the other words.

Read Aloud Explain that you will read aloud a story about a mouse that searches for the right home. Then read aloud "A New Home for Marvin Mouse." Discuss the Comprehension questions.

Day 4

Categorize and Classify

Reread and Explain Reread "A New Home for Marvin Mouse." At the end of each sentence that includes an oral vocabulary word, stop and repeat the explanation of the word. Then reread the sentence.

Use a Graphic Organizer Use the graphic organizer and the questions below to reinforce understanding of the relationship between each word and the category.

```
     Words About
     Ways to Move
        /    \
   climbing  landing
```

1. **Climbing is one way to move. What are some other words that tell about ways to move? Add these to the graphic organizer as children suggest them.** (Sample answers: walk; run; skip)

2. **What parts of your body do you move when you eat?** (Sample answer: mouth, tongue, teeth)

3. **Name a place where an animal lives.** (Sample answers: bird in a nest; fox in a den)

Day 5

Deepen Understanding

Review Repeat explanations for all oral vocabulary words. Use the definitions and examples from Day 1 and Day 3.

Guide Partner Activities Have partners work together to complete each of the activities below. Circulate and listen to partners as they work. Provide corrective feedback.

Categorize Work with a partner. Name two places that are **near** your school. Name two places that are **far** from your school.

Examples Tell a partner about the **deepest** water you have ever seen. Explain how you felt when you saw it.

Describe Talk to your partner. Tell about the **area** of your school where people **eat**.

Compare Talk to your partner. Compare the way a monkey **climbs** to the way a frog jumps and then **lands**. Show each action.

Draw Draw a picture of the place where you **live**. Tell your partner about what it is like there.

Assess To assess what word meanings children have learned, copy and distribute the **Pretest/Posttest** on pages 118–119. Use page 75 to administer the test. Compare scores with Day 1 assessment.

Unit 3, Lesson 14 • **T29**

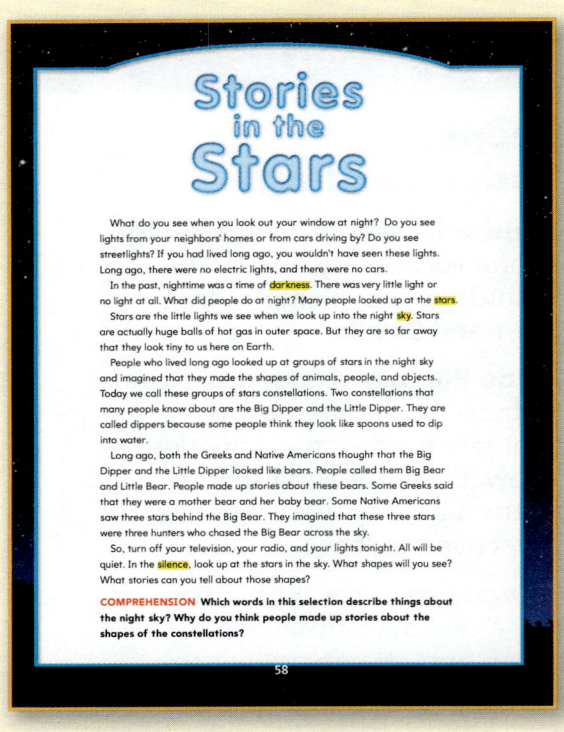

Unit 3
Lesson 15

Days 1 and 2
"Stories in the Stars," Vol. 1, pp. 58–59

Days 3 and 4
"Cloud Shapes," Vol. 1, pp. 60–61

Assessment
Pretest/Posttest Administration p. 76
Pretest/Posttest Blackline Masters pp. 120–121

T30 • Curious About Words

Day 1

Introduce Meanings

Explain To assess what word meanings children already know, copy and distribute the **Pretest/Posttest** on pages 120–121. Use page 76 to administer the test.

Explain Write each oral vocabulary word below on the board. Read it aloud. Offer an explanation and a brief example for each word.

Words About Night

darkness *n.* very little light *When Dad went in the basement, he needed a flashlight to see in the darkness.*

silence *n.* very little sound or no sound *There was silence in the classroom as the students focused on the test.*

sky *n.* the air above the ground *There are clouds in the sky today.*

stars *n.* giant balls of fire in space that are so far away they look tiny *The stars are hard to see on a cloudy night.*

Discuss Guide children to see the relationship between each word and the category. Ask: What might you see if you were outside at night? Would you hear any sounds? Prompt children to use each of the words in their answers.

Read Aloud Explain that you will read aloud a story about stars in the night sky. Then read aloud "Stories in the Stars." Discuss the Comprehension questions.

Day 2

Categorize and Classify

Reread and Explain Reread "Stories in the Stars." At the end of each sentence that includes an oral vocabulary word, stop and repeat the explanation of the word. Then reread the sentence.

Use a Graphic Organizer Use the graphic organizer and the questions below to reinforce understanding of the relationship between each word and the category.

```
        Words to Describe
         Things Above Us
        /       |        \
      sky     stars    darkness
```

1. The faint light of **stars** can usually only be seen in places where there is _____. (**darkness**)

2. Do you only hear **silence** at night? What sounds do you hear at night? What sounds do you not hear at night? (Sample answers: no; Hear: televisions, cars, trucks; Not Hear: people talking, phone ringing)

15-20 Minute Lessons

Unit 3

Lesson 15

Day 3

Introduce Meanings

Explain Write each oral vocabulary word below on the board. Read it aloud. Offer an explanation and a brief example for each word.

Words About Seeing

look *v.* to search using your eyes *Please help me look for my lost shoe.*

noticed *v.* became aware of *She noticed that the cookies had chocolate chips.*

saw *v.* used your eyes *When the baby saw the rattle, he reached for it.*

spy *v.* to find something using your eyes *I spy a butterfly in the garden.*

Discuss Guide children to see the relationship between each word and the category. Ask: What do you see in our classroom? Prompt children to use each of the words in their answers.

Read Aloud Explain that you will read aloud a story about two girls who look for shapes in the clouds. Then read aloud "Cloud Shapes." Discuss the Comprehension questions.

Day 4

Categorize and Classify

Read and Explain Reread "Cloud Shapes." At the end of each sentence that includes an oral vocabulary word, stop and repeat the explanation of the word. Then reread the sentence.

Use a Graphic Organizer Use the graphic organizer and the questions below to reinforce understanding of the relationship between each word and the category.

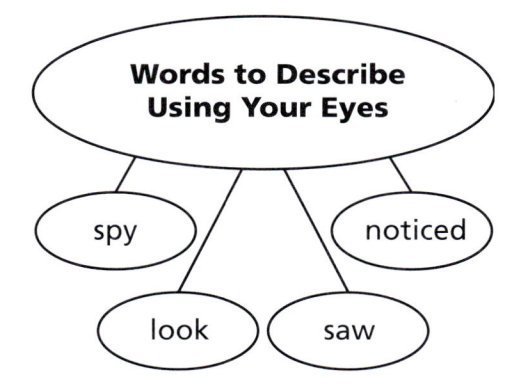

Words to Describe Using Your Eyes
- spy
- noticed
- look
- saw

1. What are some things you might **spy** on a playground? (Sample answer: a slide, swings, monkey bars)

2. What kinds of animals might you **look** at if you were at the zoo? (Sample answer: monkeys, lions)

3. What might a police officer do if he or she **noticed** a car with a flat tire? (Sample answer: He or she might call for help.)

Day 5

Deepen Understanding

Review Repeat explanations for all oral vocabulary words. Use the definitions and examples from Day 1 and Day 3.

Guide Partner Activities Have partners work together to complete each of the activities below. Circulate and listen to partners as they work. Provide corrective feedback.

Examples Name three things you might **spy** in the **sky** during the day and at night. When might you see **stars**? Tell your partner.

Role-Play Make a face like you just **noticed** that your favorite toy is missing. Then show how you might **look** around for your toy.

Describe Close your eyes. Describe what the **darkness** is like. Cover your ears. Describe what the **silence** is like. Take turns with a partner.

Draw Draw a picture of the funniest thing you ever **saw**. Tell a partner about your picture.

Assess To assess what word meanings children have learned, copy and distribute the **Pretest/Posttest** on pages 120–121. Use page 76 to administer the test. Compare scores with Day 1 assessment.

Unit 3, Lesson 15 • **T31**

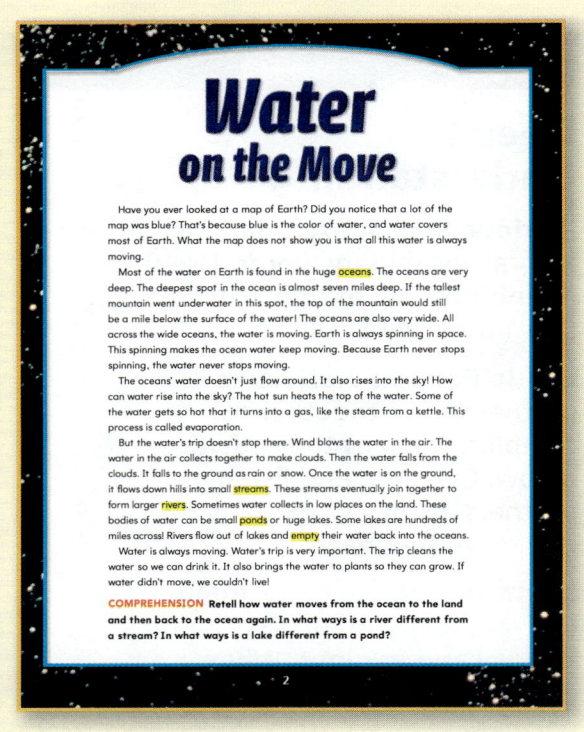

Unit 4
Lesson 16

Water on the Move

Have you ever looked at a map of Earth? Did you notice that a lot of the map was blue? That's because blue is the color of water, and water covers most of Earth. What the map does not show you is that all this water is always moving.

Most of the water on Earth is found in the huge **oceans**. The oceans are very deep. The deepest spot in the ocean is almost seven miles deep. If the tallest mountain went underwater in this spot, the top of the mountain would still be a mile below the surface of the water! The oceans are also very wide. All across the wide oceans, the water is moving. Earth is always spinning in space. This spinning makes the ocean water keep moving. Because Earth never stops spinning, the water never stops moving.

The oceans' water doesn't just flow around. It also rises into the sky! How can water rise into the sky? The hot sun heats the top of the water. Some of the water gets so hot that it turns into a gas, like the steam from a kettle. This process is called evaporation.

But the water's trip doesn't stop there. Wind blows the water in the air. The water in the air collects together to make clouds. Then the water falls from the clouds. It falls to the ground as rain or snow. Once the water is on the ground, it flows down hills into small **streams**. These streams eventually join together to form larger **rivers**. Sometimes water collects in low places on the land. These bodies of water can be small **ponds** or huge lakes. Some lakes are hundreds of miles across! Rivers flow out of lakes and **empty** their water back into the oceans.

Water is always moving. Water's trip is very important. The trip cleans the water so we can drink it. It also brings the water to plants so they can grow. If water didn't move, we couldn't live!

COMPREHENSION Retell how water moves from the ocean to the land and then back to the ocean again. In what ways is a river different from a stream? In what ways is a lake different from a pond?

2

Days 1 and 2
"Water on the Move," Vol. 2, pp. 2–3

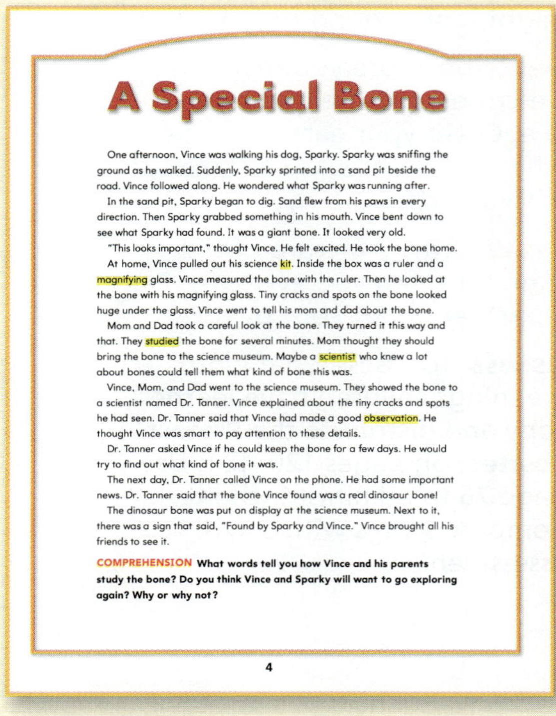

A Special Bone

One afternoon, Vince was walking his dog, Sparky. Sparky was sniffing the ground as he walked. Suddenly, Sparky sprinted into a sand pit beside the road. Vince followed along. He wondered what Sparky was running after.

In the sand pit, Sparky began to dig. Sand flew from his paws in every direction. Then Sparky grabbed something in his mouth. Vince bent down to see what Sparky had found. It was a giant bone. It looked very old.

"This looks important," thought Vince. He felt excited. He took the bone home. At home, Vince pulled out his science **kit**. Inside the box was a ruler and a **magnifying** glass. Vince measured the bone with the ruler. Then he looked at the bone with his magnifying glass. Tiny cracks and spots on the bone looked huge under the glass. Vince went to tell his mom and dad about the bone.

Mom and Dad took a careful look at the bone. They turned it this way and that. They **studied** the bone for several minutes. Mom thought they should bring the bone to the science museum. Maybe a **scientist** who knew a lot about bones could tell them what kind of bone this was.

Vince, Mom, and Dad went to the science museum. They showed the bone to a scientist named Dr. Tanner. Vince explained about the tiny cracks and spots he had seen. Dr. Tanner said that Vince had made a good **observation**. He thought Vince was smart to pay attention to these details.

Dr. Tanner asked Vince if he could keep the bone for a few days. He would try to find out what kind of bone it was.

The next day, Dr. Tanner called Vince on the phone. He had some important news. Dr. Tanner said that the bone Vince found was a real dinosaur bone!

The dinosaur bone was put on display at the science museum. Next to it, there was a sign that said, "Found by Sparky and Vince." Vince brought all his friends to see it.

COMPREHENSION What words tell you how Vince and his parents study the bone? Do you think Vince and Sparky will want to go exploring again? Why or why not?

4

Days 3 and 4
"A Special Bone," Vol. 2, pp. 4–5

Assessment
Pretest/Posttest Administration p. 77

Pretest/Posttest Blackline Masters
pp. 122–123

T32 • Curious About Words

Day 1

Introduce Meanings

Assess To assess what word meanings children already know, copy and distribute the **Pretest/Posttest** on pages 122–123. Use page 77 to administer the test.

Explain Write each oral vocabulary word below on the board. Read it aloud. Offer an explanation and a brief example for each word.

Words About Water

emptied v. flowed from one place to another *The water from the bathtub emptied into the drain.*

ocean n. a large body of salt water *Whales live in the ocean.*

pond n. a small body of water *She can swim from one side of the pond to the other.*

river n. a wide path of moving water *Many boats travel up and down the river each day.*

stream n. a narrow path of moving water *We crossed the stream on a small bridge.*

Discuss Guide children to see the relationship between each word and the category. Prompt them to talk about **ponds, streams, rivers,** or **oceans** they are familiar with. Then ask: What are three things you have emptied?

Read Aloud Explain that you will read aloud a story about where water is found on planet Earth. Then read aloud "Water on the Move." Discuss the Comprehension questions.

Day 2

Categorize and Classify

Reread and Explain Reread "Water on the Move." At the end of each sentence that includes an oral vocabulary word, stop and repeat the explanation of the word. Then reread the sentence.

Use a Graphic Organizer Use the graphic organizer and the questions below to reinforce understanding of the relationship between each word and the category. Point out that sometimes a river is very deep and sometimes it is not very deep.

Venn diagram:
- **Very, Very Deep**: ocean
- **Both**: river
- **Not Very Deep**: pond, stream

1. What are some other words for water that is very, very deep? Add these words to the graphic organizer as children suggest them. (Sample answers: lake; sea)

2. Think about this sentence: *Tara poured out a bucket of water.* Which vocabulary word tells what Tara did? (emptied)

3. Which would be harder to get across, a **stream** or a **river**? Explain why. (Sample answer: a river because it is wider and can be deeper)

15-20 Minute Lessons

Unit 4

Lesson 16

Day 3

Introduce Meanings

Explain Write each oral vocabulary word below on the board. Read it aloud. Offer an explanation and a brief example for each word.

Words About Science

kit *n.* a set of tools *The school nurse has a first-aid kit in case someone gets hurt.*

magnifying *adj.* making something look bigger *The magnifying glass helped me see the tiny bug's eyes.*

observation *n.* a careful look at something *The teacher stopped to make an observation of each plant she saw in the woods.*

scientist *n.* a person who studies nature *The scientist knows many facts about butterflies.*

studied *v.* looked at carefully *She studied the menu before ordering her lunch.*

Discuss Guide children to see the relationship between each word and the category. Ask questions such as these: What things might you find in a **scientist's kit**? What things might you look at with a **magnifying** glass?

Read Aloud Explain that you will read aloud a story about a boy and his dog who find a dinosaur bone. Then read aloud "A Special Bone." Discuss the Comprehension questions.

Day 4

Categorize and Classify

Reread and Explain Reread "A Special Bone." At the end of each sentence that includes an oral vocabulary word, stop and repeat the explanation of the word. Then reread the sentence.

Use a Graphic Organizer Use the graphic organizer and the questions below to reinforce understanding of the relationship between each word and the category.

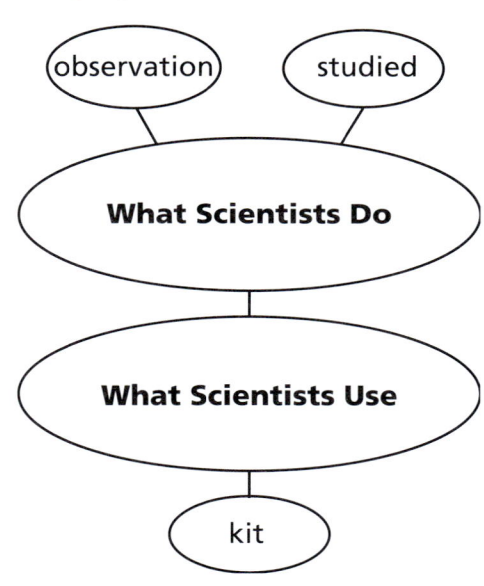

- observation
- studied

What Scientists Do

What Scientists Use

- kit

1. If you have a question about outer space, you might ask a _____. (**scientist**)

2. Why would a **magnifying** glass be a good tool to use to make an **observation** of ants? (Sample answer: The magnifying glass would make the ants look bigger.)

3. What other tools might a **scientist** use? Add these to the graphic organizer as children suggest them. (Sample answers: microscope; telescope; ruler; calculator)

Day 5

Deepen Understanding

Review Repeat explanations for all oral vocabulary words. Use the definitions and examples from Day 1 and Day 3.

Guide Partner Activities Have partners work together to complete each of the activities below. Circulate and listen to partners as they work. Provide corrective feedback.

Examples Name some animals that swim in a **pond**. Then name some places where water has **emptied** from one place to another. Tell your partner.

Role-Play Pretend you are a **scientist** visiting a classroom. Explain your job to your partner. Use these words: **magnifying, observation, kit, studied**.

Describe Work with your partner. Describe what you could do to have fun at a **stream**. Then describe what you could do to have fun at a **river**.

Draw Draw a picture of something you might find in the **ocean**. Share your picture with your partner.

Assess To assess what word meanings children have learned, copy and distribute the **Pretest/Posttest** on pages 122–123. Use page 77 to administer the test. Compare scores with Day 1 assessment.

Unit 4, Lesson 16 • **T33**

Unit 4
Lesson 17

Peaches and Bees

Days 1 and 2
"Peaches and Bees," Vol. 2, pp. 6–7

What's in the Field?

Days 3 and 4
"What's in the Field?" Vol. 2, pp. 8–9

Assessment
Pretest/Posttest Administration p. 78

Pretest/Posttest Blackline Masters pp. 124–125

T34 • Curious About Words

Day 1

Introduce Meanings

Assess To assess what word meanings children already know, copy and distribute the **Pretest/Posttest** on pages 124–125. Use page 78 to administer the test.

Explain Write each oral vocabulary word below on the board. Read it aloud. Offer an explanation and a brief example for each word.

Words About Nature

branches *n.* parts of a tree that grow out from the trunk *Some of the branches of the tree were high off the ground.*

environment *n.* all of the things around where someone or something lives *Frogs live in an environment with water, rocks, and plants.*

insects *n.* small animals with six legs and usually wings *Butterflies are insects.*

leaves *n.* flat, thin parts of a tree *The leaves on the tree turned red in the fall.*

soil *n.* dirt *Garden plants need good soil to grow in.*

Discuss Guide children to see the relationship between each word and the category. If possible, point outside to a tree and prompt them to describe the tree and its **environment**. If not possible, ask them to close their eyes and imagine trees and what surrounds them, before describing them.

Read Aloud Explain that you will read aloud a story about how bees and fruit trees work together in nature. Then read aloud "Peaches and Bees." Discuss the Comprehension questions.

Day 2

Categorize and Classify

Reread and Explain Reread "Peaches and Bees." At the end of each sentence that includes an oral vocabulary word, stop and repeat the explanation of the word. Then reread the sentence.

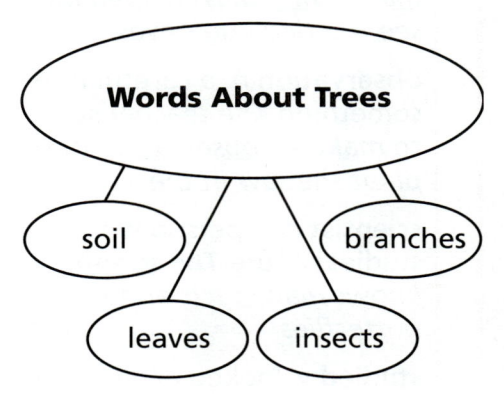

Use a Graphic Organizer Use the graphic organizer and the questions below to reinforce understanding of the relationship between each word and the category.

Words About Trees
- soil
- branches
- leaves
- insects

1. A tree starts its life as a seed in the _____. (**soil**)
2. Where might you find **leaves**? (Sample answers: on tree branches; on plants; on the ground)
3. Why do some birds live in an **environment** with trees? (Sample answer: so they can build nests in trees and find food)

15-20 Minute Lessons

Unit 4

Lesson 17

Day 3

Introduce Meanings

Explain Write each oral vocabulary word below on the board. Read it aloud. Offer an explanation and a brief example for each word.

More Words About Nature

breeze *n.* a light wind *The breeze hardly moved the branches on the tree.*

cloud *n.* a shape in the sky made of drops of water *Rain fell from the dark cloud over the town.*

exploration *n.* a look at a place to see what is there *The sisters went on an exploration of their new neighborhood.*

field *n.* a large area of land *The horses eat grass in the field.*

plant *n.* a living thing that grows in soil *They will pick strawberries from that plant.*

Discuss Guide children to see the relationship between each word and the category. Ask questions such as these: What might you find on an **exploration** of a **field**? What does a **breeze** feel like? Have you ever looked for shapes in the **clouds**?

Read Aloud Explain that you will read aloud a story about a sister and brother who explore nature together. Then read aloud "What's in the Field?" Discuss the Comprehension questions.

Day 4

Categorize and Classify

Reread and Explain Reread "What's in the Field?" At the end of each sentence that includes an oral vocabulary word, stop and repeat the explanation of the word. Then reread the sentence.

Use a Graphic Organizer Use the graphic organizer and the questions below to reinforce understanding of the relationship between each word and the category.

Words About Things on the Ground	Words About Things in the Air
field plant	cloud breeze

1. Name some animals you might see in a **field** on a farm. (Sample answers: horses, cows, sheep)

2. What colors are **clouds**? (Sample answers: white, gray, black)

3. Think about this sentence: *Danielle could not get her kite off the ground in the light breeze.* Why wouldn't Danielle's kite fly? (Sample answer: The wind was not strong enough to lift the kite.)

4. Where might be a fun place to go on an **exploration**? Why? (Sample answer: the woods, because you could discover all kinds of plants and bugs there)

Day 5

Deepen Understanding

Review Repeat explanations for all oral vocabulary words. Use the definitions and examples from Day 1 and Day 3.

Guide Partner Activities Have partners work together to complete each of the activities below. Circulate and listen to partners as they work. Provide corrective feedback.

Categorize Work with a partner. Name three things in the classroom **environment**. Then name three places to go on an **exploration**. Tell which place would be your first choice.

Examples What are some **insects** you have seen? Tell your partner.

Role-Play Show how you would look if a rain **cloud** showed up during a picnic. Now show how you would look if a **breeze** blew the cloud away.

Describe Talk to your partner. Describe a **field** near where you live. What grows there? What lives there?

Draw Draw a picture of a **plant** growing in **soil**. Include **leaves** on the plant. Share your picture with a partner and tell about it.

Discuss Work with a partner. Create a story about an animal that lives in the **branches** of a tree. Draw a picture to go with your story.

Assess To assess what word meanings children have learned, copy and distribute the **Pretest/Posttest** on pages 124–125. Use page 78 to administer the test. Compare scores with Day 1 assessment.

Unit 4, Lesson 17 • **T35**

Unit 4
Lesson 18

A Scavenger Hunt at the Seashore

Days 1 and 2
"A Scavenger Hunt at the Seashore," Vol. 2, pp. 10–11

In One Big Red Bucket

Days 3 and 4
"In One Big Red Bucket," Vol. 2, pp. 12–13

Assessment
Pretest/Posttest Administration p. 79

Pretest/Posttest Blackline Masters pp. 126–127

T36 • Curious About Words

Day 1

Introduce Meanings

Assess To assess what word meanings children already know, copy and distribute the **Pretest/Posttest** on pages 126–127. Use page 79 to administer the test.

Explain Write each oral vocabulary word below on the board. Read it aloud. Offer an explanation and a brief example for each word.

Words About Places

here *adv.* at this place *Please sit here next to the window.*

high *adv.* way up *The bird flies high in the sky.*

land *n.* the part of Earth not covered by water *Some turtles live only on land.*

places *n.* where things are *It is fun to explore new places.*

sand *n.* many tiny pieces of rock *The sand on the beach was soft under our feet.*

Discuss Guide children to see the relationship between each word and the category. Ask questions such as these: What are your favorite **places** to visit? Have you ever walked on the **sand** at a beach? If so, what did you see on the sand?

Read Aloud Explain that you will read aloud a story about some places where animals are found at the seashore. Then read aloud "A Scavenger Hunt at the Seashore." Discuss the Comprehension questions.

Day 2

Categorize and Classify

Reread and Explain Reread "A Scavenger Hunt at the Seashore." At the end of each sentence that includes an oral vocabulary word, stop and repeat the explanation of the word. Then reread the sentence.

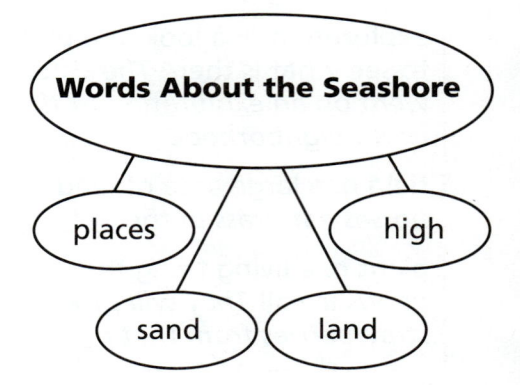

Use a Graphic Organizer Use the graphic organizer and the questions below to reinforce understanding of the relationship between each word and the category.

Words About the Seashore
- places
- high
- sand
- land

1. Name two **places** where animals live at the seashore. (Sample answer: in the water, on **land**)

2. Waves in the ocean can get very _____. (**high**)

3. The crab crawled from there to _____. (**here**)

15-20 Minute Lessons

Unit 4

Lesson 18

Day 3

Introduce Meanings

Explain Write each oral vocabulary word below on the board. Read it aloud. Offer an explanation and a brief example for each word.

Words About Numbers

one *adj.* a single thing *A rabbit has <u>one</u> tail.*

two *adj.* one more than one *A bicycle has <u>two</u> wheels.*

three *adj.* one more than two *There are <u>three</u> letters in the word fun.*

four *adj.* one more than three *A car has <u>four</u> wheels.*

five *adj.* one more than four *This star has <u>five</u> points.*

Discuss Guide children to see the relationship between each word and the category. Have them use the words to count objects in the classroom. You may choose to have children use math manipulatives to model the numbers.

Read Aloud Explain that you will read aloud a story about the number of animals two brothers find at a lake. Then read aloud "In One Big Red Bucket." Discuss the Comprehension questions.

Day 4

Categorize and Classify

Reread and Explain Reread "In One Big Red Bucket." At the end of each sentence that includes an oral vocabulary word, stop and repeat the explanation of the word. Then reread the sentence.

Use a Graphic Organizer Use the graphic organizer and the questions below to reinforce understanding of the relationship between each word and the category.

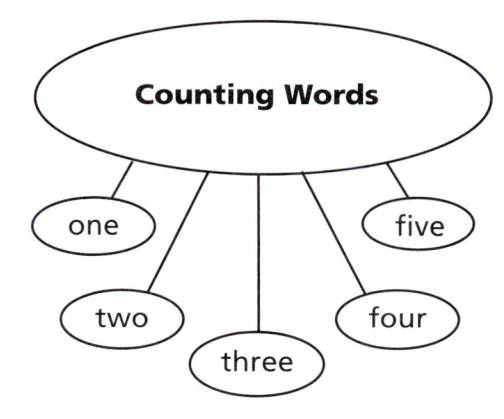

Counting Words
- one
- two
- three
- four
- five

1. How many noses does a cat have? How many eyes does it have? **(one; two)**
2. How many fingers do you have on one hand? **(five)**
3. How many legs does a dog have? **(four)**
4. If you color a picture red, white, and blue, how many colors will you use? **(three)**

Day 5

Deepen Understanding

Review Repeat explanations for all oral vocabulary words. Use the definitions and examples from Day 1 and Day 3.

Guide Partner Activities Have partners work together to complete each of the activities below. Circulate and listen to partners as they work. Provide corrective feedback.

Describe Work with a partner. Tell about a trip to the beach. Describe what you would see lying on the **sand**.

Role-Play Imagine you can fly **high** over the **land**. Tell your partner about **five places** you see.

Draw Draw a snowman with **three** body parts, **two** eyes, and **one** nose. Draw **four** buttons on the snowman. Tell your partner about your picture using the number words.

Discuss Work with a partner. Create sentences about things at school. Use the word **here** in each sentence.

Assess To assess what word meanings children have learned, copy and distribute the **Pretest/Posttest** on pages 126–127. Use page 79 to administer the test. Compare scores with Day 1 assessment.

Unit 4, Lesson 18 • **T37**

Unit 4
Lesson 19

Hiking for Blueberries

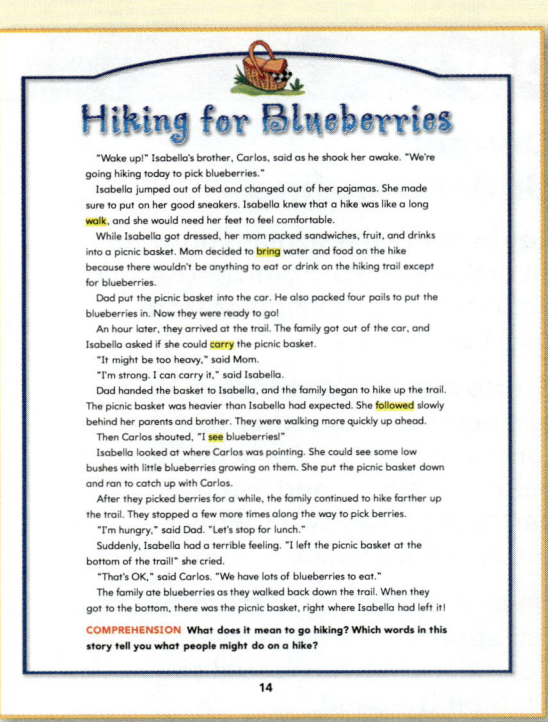

Days 1 and 2

"Hiking for Blueberries," Vol. 2, pp. 14–15

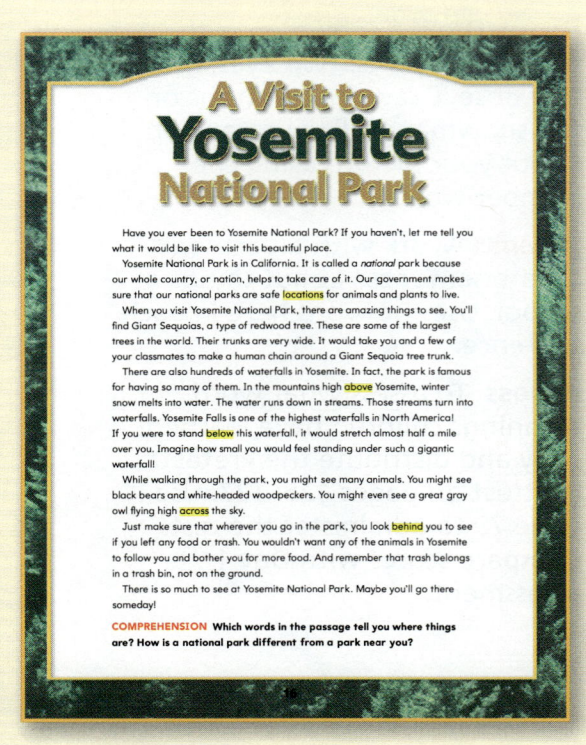

A Visit to Yosemite National Park

Days 3 and 4

"A Visit to Yosemite National Park," Vol. 2, pp. 16–17

Assessment

Pretest/Posttest Administration p. 80

Pretest/Posttest Blackline Masters pp. 128–129

T38 • Curious About Words

Day 1

Introduce Meanings

Assess To assess what word meanings children already know, copy and distribute the **Pretest/Posttest** on pages 128–129. Use page 80 to administer the test.

Explain Write each oral vocabulary word below on the board. Read it aloud. Offer an explanation and a brief example for each word.

Words About Hiking

bring *v.* to take something with you *Mom will bring water for everybody.*

carry *v.* to hold and take something from one place to another *Dad will carry the lunches.*

follow *v.* to go behind *The children follow their dad on the walking trail.*

see *v.* to use the eyes to notice things *They see a squirrel in a tree.*

walk *n.* going somewhere on foot *The family went for a long walk in the woods.*

Discuss Guide children to see the relationship between each word and the category. Ask questions such as these: Have you ever taken a long **walk** with your family? Where did you go? What did you **bring** with you? What did you **see**?

Read Aloud Explain that you will read aloud a story about a family who goes on a hike. Then read aloud "Hiking for Blueberries." Discuss the Comprehension questions.

Day 2

Categorize and Classify

Reread and Explain Reread "Hiking for Blueberries." At the end of each sentence that includes an oral vocabulary word, stop and repeat the explanation of the word. Then reread the sentence.

Use a Graphic Organizer Use the graphic organizer and the questions below to reinforce understanding of the relationship between each word and the category.

Words About Using Your Legs	Words About Using Your Arms
walk follow	carry bring

1. When you take a **walk**, you move with your legs. What are some other ways to move with your legs? Add these to the graphic organizer as children suggest them. (Sample answers: run; hop; skip)

2. When you **carry** a box, you use your arms. What are some other ways to use your arms? Add these to the graphic organizer as children suggest them. (Sample answers: wave; throw; hug)

3. Name some things you **see** in the classroom. (Sample answer: tables, chairs, shapes, letters, fish)

15-20 Minute Lessons

Unit 4

Lesson 19

Day 3

Introduce Meanings

Explain Write each oral vocabulary word below on the board. Read it aloud. Offer an explanation and a brief example for each word.

Words That Tell Where
above *prep.* over *The ceiling is above us.*
across *prep.* to the other side of *She kicked the ball across the playground.*
behind *prep.* in back of *What is behind the school?*
below *prep.* under *The floor is below us.*
location *n.* the place where something is *The library is a good location to read a book.*

Discuss Guide children to see the relationship between each word and the category. Ask questions such as these: Where at school is a good **location** to play a game of tag? What do you see **across** the classroom? Who sits **behind** you?

Read Aloud Explain that you will read aloud a story about where to find places in a special park. Then read aloud "A Visit to Yosemite National Park." Discuss the Comprehension questions.

Day 4

Categorize and Classify

Reread and Explain Reread "A Visit to Yosemite National Park." At the end of each sentence that includes an oral vocabulary word, stop and repeat the explanation of the word. Then reread the sentence.

Use a Graphic Organizer Use the graphic organizer and the questions below to reinforce understanding of the relationship between each word and the category.

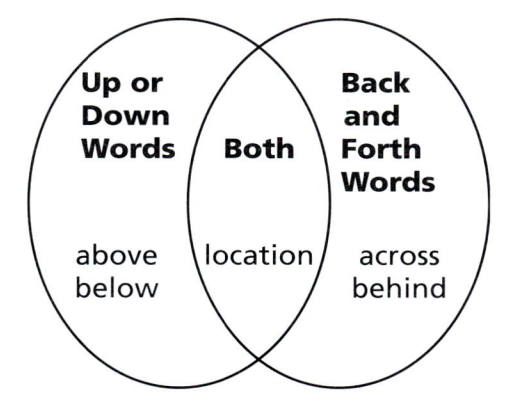

Up or Down Words: above, below
Both: location
Back and Forth Words: across, behind

1. What word tells where the person in back of you sits? (behind)
2. Name the **location** in school where you eat lunch. Name a location in school where you sing songs. (Sample answers: cafeteria; classroom)
3. Name something you see **across** the classroom. Is it close to you or far away from you? (Answers will vary.)

Day 5

Deepen Understanding

Review Repeat explanations for all oral vocabulary words. Use the definitions and examples from Day 1 and Day 3.

Guide Partner Activities Have partners work together to complete each of the activities below. Circulate and listen to partners as they work. Provide corrective feedback.

Categorize Work with your partner. Name three things you might **see above** your head. Then name three things you might see **below** your feet.

Role-Play Show how you would **carry** a full plate of spaghetti **across** the room.

Examples What are some things you might find **behind** a closet door? Tell your partner.

Describe Describe a **location** where you have fun. Tell your partner about the place.

Draw Draw a picture of something you would **bring** on a long **walk**. Tell your partner about your picture.

Discuss Talk to your partner. Tell how to play the game "Follow the Leader." Use the word **follow**.

Assess To assess what word meanings children have learned, copy and distribute the **Pretest/Posttest** on pages 128–129. Use page 80 to administer the test. Compare scores with Day 1 assessment.

Unit 4, Lesson 19 • **T39**

Unit 4
Lesson 20

Ferdinand Magellan Explores the World

One of the greatest **journeys** ever taken was a trip by Ferdinand Magellan. He tried to sail all the way around the **world**.

Today we know that the world—our Earth—is round like a ball. We know that if you start in one place and keep moving in the same direction, you can **go** all the way around the world. You can end your trip right where you began it! But hundreds of years ago, some people thought the world was flat like a plate. Those people thought that if Magellan sailed too far across the world, he would fall right off the edge! But they were wrong.

In 1519, Magellan began his journey in a **country** called Spain. Spain had a king named Charles. King Charles wanted Magellan to sail west to a place called the Spice Islands. Magellan took five boats with him and many men to sail those boats. They sailed west. It was Magellan's job to tell the men how to sail across the oceans. This was a hard job. Sometimes the boats got lost.

There was also bad weather. The weather was at its worst when Magellan sailed around the bottom tip of South America. One of his boats sank. Men on another boat got scared and went back to Spain. But Magellan kept going. Next, he sailed across the Pacific Ocean. For about one hundred days, Magellan's boats were far **away** from land and people. The sailors started to run out of food and water. But then they made it to land and got more food and water.

Magellan could not finish the trip around the world. But the sailors of one of his boats made it to the Spice Islands and then sailed home to Spain. They had finished the first journey around the world!

COMPREHENSION What words about travel help you understand Ferdinand Magellan's trip around the world? What made Magellan's journey hard?

18

Days 1 and 2

"Ferdinand Magellan Explores the World," Vol. 2, pp. 18–19

Exploring for Treasure

Tom and Joe are best friends. They play lots of games together. But most of all, they like to play pirates.

Once, when Tom and Joe were playing pirates, they decided to explore for real buried treasure. Soon after the boys started digging, Joe's dog, Milo, came to help. Milo began digging so wildly that the boys thought he must have buried a bone there. Bones were buried all around the yard, and **whenever** Milo started digging like this, he **always** found one. But not this time! Before long, the boys realized that Milo had found something better than a bone.

"Look!" exclaimed Tom. "That's not a bone!" Milo had dug up a box. Tom picked it up. The box was made of brown leather with gold trim. There was a tiny padlock on the front. "I've **never** seen anything like this," said Tom.

"It must be real treasure!" said Joe.

The boys raced into the house and asked Joe's mom for help. "I have a special key that might open it," she said.

Joe tried the key and the padlock opened! The boys opened the lid slowly, imagining the beautiful gems and gold coins they would find inside. But all they saw was an old newspaper, a dollar bill, and a doll. They were disappointed. "What's this?" asked Tom. "This isn't buried treasure."

"Yes it is," Joe's mother explained. "It's just a different kind of treasure. It's a time capsule. Someone must have buried it **years** ago. To make a time capsule, people put things from a certain time period into a container. Then they bury it so other people can find it later and learn about what things were like during that time."

"Wow," said Tom. "That's neat!"

"Yeah," said Joe. "Let's add some things to this time capsule and make our own buried treasure!"

COMPREHENSION Which words tell about how often things happen? What makes the boys' discovery so exciting?

20

Days 3 and 4

"Exploring for Treasure," Vol. 2, pp. 20–21

Assessment

Pretest/Posttest Administration p. 81

Pretest/Posttest Blackline Masters pp. 130–131

T40 • Curious About Words

Day 1

Introduce Meanings

Assess To assess what word meanings children already know, copy and distribute the **Pretest/Posttest** on pages 130–131. Use page 81 to administer the test.

Explain Write each oral vocabulary word below on the board. Read it aloud. Offer an explanation and a brief example for each word.

Words About Travel

away *adv.* not here *The seashore is far away from her home.*

country *n.* a land where people live *The United States is a country.*

go *v.* to move from one place to another *We will go on a long trip.*

journey *n.* a trip *The man brought food for the long journey ahead.*

world *n.* the earth *Around the world, people live in many kinds of homes.*

Discuss Guide children to see the relationship between each word and the category. Ask questions such as these: What words would you use to talk about a trip someone took? Have you ever been far **away** from home? Name a **country** you would like to visit.

Read Aloud Explain that you will read aloud a story about a man who tried to sail around the world. Then read aloud "Ferdinand Magellan Explores the World." Discuss the Comprehension questions.

Day 2

Categorize and Classify

Reread and Explain Reread "Ferdinand Magellan Explores the World." At the end of each sentence that includes an oral vocabulary word, stop and repeat the explanation of the word. Then reread the sentence.

Use a Graphic Organizer Use the graphic organizer and the questions below to reinforce understanding of the relationship between each word and the category.

Places: world, country
Both: away
Taking a Trip: go, journey

1. It can take many hours to get to a **country** that is far _____. (away)

2. How might someone **go** to a **country** that is across the ocean? (Sample answers: by plane; by boat)

3. Name somewhere you would like to go on a **journey**. (Sample answers: a friend's house far away; a rainforest)

Unit 4

Lesson 20

15-20 Minute Lessons

Day 3

Introduce Meanings

Explain Write each oral vocabulary word below on the board. Read it aloud. Offer an explanation and a brief example for each word.

Words About Time

always *adv.* every time *Grandma always calls me on my birthday.*

never *adv.* not ever *Earth never stops spinning.*

once *adv.* one time only *She walks her dog once a day.*

whenever *conj.* at any time *He likes to ride his skateboard whenever he can.*

years *n.* the times between each of your birthdays; periods of 365 days *The boy is nine years old.*

Discuss Guide children to see the relationship between each word and the category. Prompt them to use the words to tell about things they **always** do and things they **never** do.

Read Aloud Explain that you will read aloud a story about two boys who find a treasure from years ago. Then read aloud "Exploring for Treasure." Discuss the Comprehension questions.

Day 4

Categorize and Classify

Reread and Explain Reread "Exploring for Treasure." At the end of each sentence that includes an oral vocabulary word, stop and repeat the explanation of the word. Then reread the sentence.

Use a Graphic Organizer Use the graphic organizer and the questions below to reinforce understanding of the relationship between each word and the category.

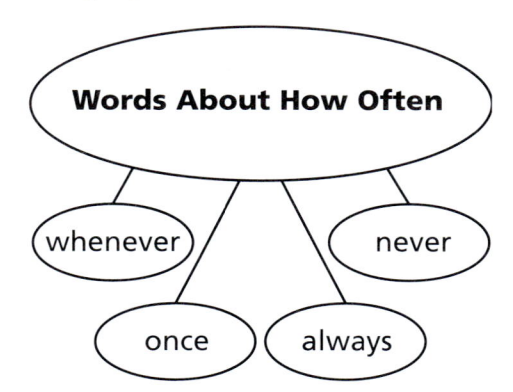

Words About How Often
- whenever
- never
- once
- always

1. How many **years** old are you? (Sample answer: six years old)
2. Your seventh birthday will happen _____. (**once**)
3. What **always** happens on your birthday? (Sample answer: I always am one year older.)
4. What other words tell how many times something happens? Add these to the graphic organizer as children suggest them. (Sample answers: sometimes; few)

Day 5

Deepen Understanding

Review Repeat explanations for all oral vocabulary words. Use the definitions and examples from Day 1 and Day 3.

Guide Partner Activities Have partners work together to complete each of the activities below. Circulate and listen to partners as they work. Provide corrective feedback.

Categorize Work with your partner. Name three things that are far **away.** Then name three things that are **always** near you. Name the one thing you would **never** want to be without.

Role-Play Pretend you are about to **go** around the **world.** What would you pack for the **journey**? Tell your partner.

Describe Talk to your partner. Describe what you like to do **whenever** you have free time.

Compare Compare your age with the age of a friend, sister, brother, or cousin. Use the word **years.** Tell your partner.

Examples Take turns with your partner. Tell what you know about the **country** you live in.

Discuss Work with your partner. Tell a story that begins with these words: *Once upon a time.*

Assess To assess what word meanings children have learned, copy and distribute the **Pretest/Posttest** on pages 130–131. Use page 81 to administer the test. Compare scores with Day 1 assessment.

Unit 4, Lesson 20 • **T41**

Unit 5
Lesson 21

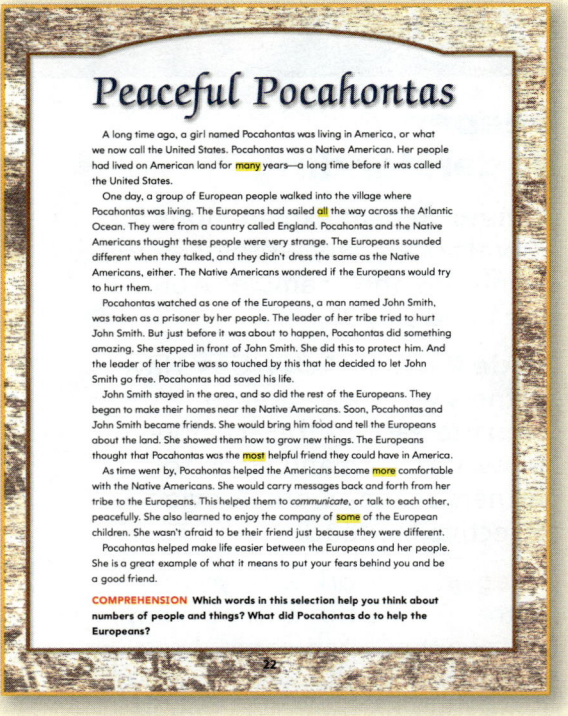

Days 1 and 2

"Peaceful Pocahontas," Vol. 2, pp. 22–23

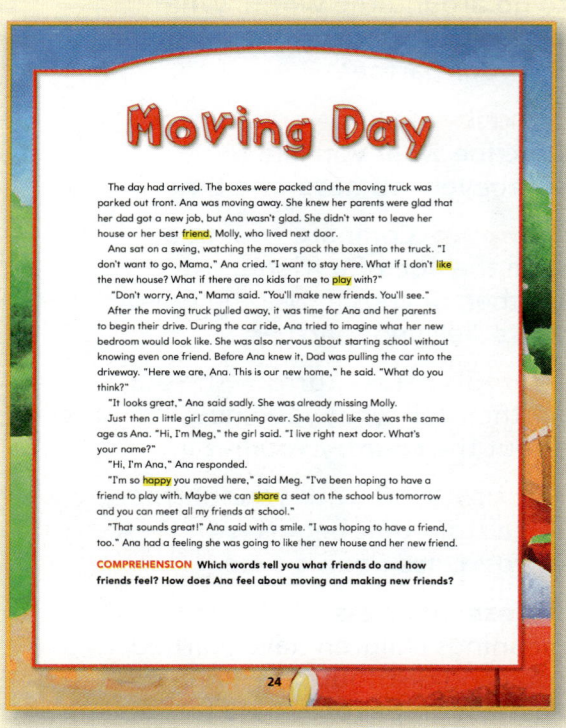

Days 3 and 4

"Moving Day," Vol. 2, pp. 24–25

Assessment

Pretest/Posttest Administration p. 82

Pretest/Posttest Blackline Masters pp. 132–133

T42 • Curious About Words

Day 1

Introduce Meanings

Assess To assess what word meanings children already know, copy and distribute the **Pretest/Posttest** on pages 132–133. Use page 82 to administer the test.

Explain Write each oral vocabulary word below on the board. Read it aloud. Offer an explanation and a brief example for each word.

Words That Tell How Much
all *adj.* every *All* the leaves fell from the tree.
many *adj.* a lot *Many* people are at the shopping mall today.
more *adj.* added; larger number or amount *We had more fun at the park today than we did yesterday.*
most *adj.* largest part, number, or amount *The library has the most books of any place I know.*
some *adj.* a few but not all *Mom planted some seeds in the garden.*

Discuss Guide children to see the relationship between each word and the category. Hand out varying quantities of objects to them. Then have them use the words to discuss how much of a given object each child has.

Read Aloud Explain that you will read aloud a story about how a girl named Pocahontas helped people a long time ago. Then read aloud "Peaceful Pocahontas." Discuss the Comprehension questions.

Day 2

Categorize and Classify

Reread and Explain Reread "Peaceful Pocahontas." At the end of each sentence that includes an oral vocabulary word, stop and repeat the explanation of the word. Then reread the sentence.

Use a Graphic Organizer Use the graphic organizer and the questions below to reinforce understanding of the relationship between each word and the category.

Words About a Lot	Words About Not a Lot
all many most	some

1. **Some** is a word you can use when you don't have a lot. What are some more words for not a lot? Add these to the graphic organizer as children suggest them. (Sample answers: few; none; little)

2. Could you have **more** toys than someone else but still not have a lot of toys? Why do you think so? (Sample answer: Yes. Two toys is more than one toy but still not a lot.)

3. Mark has **many** toys and nobody else has any. What word tells how many toys Mark has? (**all**)

15-20 Minute Lessons

Unit 5

Lesson 21

Day 3

Introduce Meanings

Explain Write each oral vocabulary word below on the board. Read it aloud. Offer an explanation and a brief example for each word.

Words About Friends

friend *n.* someone you know and like *My best friend and I like to ride bikes.*

happy *adj.* feeling good *I am happy that you are my friend.*

like *v.* to enjoy *Ben and Maria like to draw.*

play *v.* to do something fun *Can we play in the yard today?*

share *v.* to let someone have part of what you have or let someone use something you have *My friend and I will share my lunch.*

Discuss Guide children to see the relationship between each word and the category. Ask questions such as these: Who is your best friend? What games do you like to play together?

Read Aloud Explain that you will read aloud a story about a girl who made a new friend when she moved. Then read aloud "Moving Day." Discuss the Comprehension questions.

Day 4

Categorize and Classify

Reread and Explain Reread "Moving Day." At the end of each sentence that includes an oral vocabulary word, stop and repeat the explanation of the word. Then reread the sentence.

Use a Graphic Organizer Use the graphic organizer and the questions below to reinforce understanding of the relationship between each word and the category.

Words About How Friends Feel	Words About What Friends Do
happy	share play like

1. What are some other words for games you **like** to **play** with your **friends**? Add new words to the graphic organizer as children suggest them. (Sample answers: swim; draw)

2. Getting a present from a **friend** would make you feel _____. (**happy**)

3. What are two things you could **share** with someone? (Sample answer: a sandwich, a toy)

Day 5

Deepen Understanding

Review Repeat explanations for all oral vocabulary words. Use the definitions and examples from Day 1 and Day 3.

Guide Partner Activities Have partners work together to complete each of the activities below. Circulate and listen to partners as they work. Provide corrective feedback.

Categorize List two things that you think are **more** fun to do than watching television. Then list two things that you think are less fun to do than watching television.

Examples Fill in the blanks. "Many _____ **like** to _____. For example, Many cats like to purr.

Describe Talk to your partner. Describe the thing you want **most** to do during summer vacation, and why.

Draw Draw a picture of yourself **playing** with a **friend**. Then draw a picture of you and your friend **sharing** something.

Role-Play Think of **some** things you do that make you **happy**. Then act them **all** out for your classmates to guess.

Assess To assess what word meanings children have learned, copy and distribute the **Pretest/Posttest** on pages 132–133. Use page 82 to administer the test. Compare scores with Day 1 assessment.

Unit 5, Lesson 21 • **T43**

Unit 5
Lesson 22

Dinosaur Shapes and Sizes

Millions of years ago, before there were humans on Earth, there were dinosaurs. When most people think of dinosaurs, they think of their huge **size**. But not all dinosaurs were the same size. Some dinosaurs were small, and some dinosaurs were giant. Plus, some dinosaurs flew in the air and others walked on the ground. Some dinosaurs ate meat and others ate plants. Scientists are still not sure how many kinds of dinosaurs there were, but they do know that each one was **different** from the next.

Diplodocus was a very big dinosaur. It was over 120 feet long. That's longer than three school buses parked one behind the other! Diplodocus had a wide body, a long tail, a long neck, and a small head. Diplodocus walked on four legs and used its long neck to reach the plants it ate.

Tyrannosaurus rex, or T. rex, was over forty feet long and twenty feet tall. It was one of the biggest meat-eating dinosaurs. That means it hunted and ate other dinosaurs. Tyrannosaurus rex was **shaped** differently than Diplodocus. Because it needed to be able to run fast to catch other dinosaurs, Tyrannosaurus rex walked on two long legs. It also had a big head and razor-sharp teeth.

Ankylosaurus was a slow-moving dinosaur. It was about thirty-five feet long, like T. rex, but only four feet high. That's only a little bigger than you! Ankylosaurus ate only plants, so it didn't need to be big enough to hunt other dinosaurs. But it still needed to be able to protect itself from bigger, meat-eating dinosaurs like Tyrannosaurus rex. So Ankylosaurus had **tough** plates on its back, like a turtle's shell. This hard covering kept it safe.

Lesothosaurus was one of the smallest dinosaurs. It was only about three feet long. It walked on two feet, like a T. rex, and ate plants, like an Ankylosaurus. Lesothosaurus was **weaker** than most other dinosaurs. It was not strong enough to fight them and win. But Lesothosaurus was a very fast runner. It was faster than many of the big dinosaurs. It could run away to save itself.

Dinosaurs aren't living on Earth anymore, but scientists have been able to find old dinosaurs in the ground. Visit a museum sometime to see the shapes and sizes of these creatures yourself!

COMPREHENSION What words in this selection tell about the dinosaurs' bodies? How did the dinosaurs' shapes and sizes help them survive?

26

Days 1 and 2
"Dinosaur Shapes and Sizes," Vol. 2, pp. 26–27

Little Puppy Learns to Be a Kitten

One day, a farmer's little girl put her puppy on a leash and walked it outside. Right away, the puppy began to **pull** her. The puppy pulled very hard. He pulled so hard that the leash broke. And once he was free, the puppy **hopped** into a field of corn.

"**Come** back to me, puppy! Don't run away!" cried the little girl. But the puppy was already gone.

The puppy kept running, all by himself. Soon he came to a big red barn. The puppy went inside. There, he found three little kittens. The puppy wanted to play with them.

He tried to play with the first kitten. The puppy rolled on the ground and pushed the first kitten with his paws. He only meant to play. But the puppy was much bigger than the kitten. He pushed the kitten too hard, and it fell into a bowl of milk. The kitten meowed and went to hide under a pile of hay.

So the puppy tried to ask the second kitten to play. He did this by barking loudly. This frightened the kitten. Instead of playing with the puppy, the kitten **turned** around and ran away from him.

The third kitten was the last one left for the puppy to play with. It was the littlest kitten of all. It was trying to **reach** a feather. The feather was up on a shelf. It was too high for the little kitten to get to. It was not too high for the puppy to reach, though. So he reached up and pushed the feather off the shelf. It floated down. Both the littlest kitten and the puppy tried to catch it. Soon they were playing. They took turns grabbing the feather and chasing each other. Afterward, they were so tired that they both fell asleep in a pile of hay.

A while later, the farmer's little girl found her puppy sleeping with the kitten. "Look at that!" she laughed. "My puppy thinks he's a kitten!"

COMPREHENSION Which action words describe what happens in this story? Why does the littlest kitten decide to play with the puppy?

28

Days 3 and 4
"Little Puppy Learns to Be a Kitten," Vol. 2, pp. 28–29

Assessment
Pretest/Posttest Administration p. 83
Pretest/Posttest Blackline Masters pp. 134–135

T44 • Curious About Words

Day 1

Introduce Meanings

Assess To assess what word meanings children already know, copy and distribute the **Pretest/Posttest** on pages 134–135. Use page 83 to administer the test.

Explain Write each oral vocabulary word below on the board. Read it aloud. Offer an explanation and a brief example for each word.

Words to Describe Animals

different *adj.* not the same *A cat is different from a dog.*

shaped *adj.* formed or made in a certain way *The little snake was shaped like a round tube.*

size *n.* how big or small something is *A whale is huge in size.*

tough *adj.* strong and hard *A turtle's shell is tough.*

weaker *adj.* not as strong *A mouse is weaker than a cat.*

Discuss Guide children to see the relationship between each word and the category. Tell them to name some animals. Ask them questions such as these: What is **different** about each animal? Which animals are big in **size**? Which animals are small in size?

Read Aloud Explain that you will read aloud a story about different kinds of dinosaurs. Then read aloud "Dinosaur Shapes and Sizes." Discuss the Comprehension questions.

Day 2

Categorize and Classify

Reread and Explain Reread "Dinosaur Shapes and Sizes." At the end of each sentence that includes an oral vocabulary word, stop and repeat the explanation of the word. Then reread the sentence.

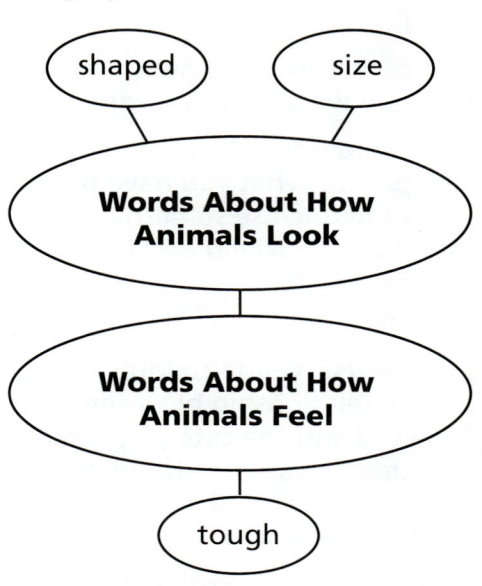

Use a Graphic Organizer Use the graphic organizer and the questions below to reinforce understanding of the relationship between each word and the category.

```
  shaped        size
      \        /
       \      /
    Words About How
    Animals Look
          |
          |
    Words About How
    Animals Feel
          |
        tough
```

1. What are some other words you can use to describe how an animal feels? Add these to the graphic organizer as children suggest them. (Sample answers: hairy; smooth; slippery)

2. Put these animals in order from smallest **size** to largest size: elephant, cat, mouse. (mouse, cat, elephant)

3. Think about animals of **different** sizes. Is a small animal always **weaker** than a large one? Explain why or why not. (Answers will vary.)

15-20 Minute Lessons

Unit 5
Lesson 22

Day 3

Introduce Meanings

Explain Write each oral vocabulary word below on the board. Read it aloud. Offer an explanation and a brief example for each word.

Words About How Things Move

come *v.* to go to something *Please come to the table for dinner.*

hop *v.* to jump over *The rabbit will hop over the small yellow flowers.*

pull *v.* to move something by tugging it toward you *I can pull the wagon up the hill.*

reach *v.* to get to something *I tried to reach the toys on the top shelf.*

turned *v.* moved around to look another way *I turned around and went back in the house.*

Discuss Guide children to see the relationship between each word and the category. Ask: What do you like to do at recess? Prompt them to use the words.

Read Aloud Explain that you will read aloud a story about a puppy that tries to become friends with three kittens. Then read aloud "Little Puppy Learns to Be a Kitten." Discuss the Comprehension questions.

Day 4

Categorize and Classify

Reread and Explain Reread "Little Puppy Learns to Be a Kitten." At the end of each sentence that includes an oral vocabulary word, stop and repeat the explanation of the word. Then reread the sentence.

Use a Graphic Organizer Use the graphic organizer and the questions below to reinforce understanding of the relationship between each word and the category.

Moving With Your Arms and Hands	Moving With Your Legs and Feet
reach pull	come turned hop

1. What word might you use to describe making many small jumps? (**hop**)
2. What are three things you might move by **pulling**? (Sample answer: a wagon, a rope, a door)
3. What word might you use to describe trying to get something that is far away from you? (**reach**)
4. Where can you **come** to see animals? (Sample answers: a farm; a zoo; a circus)

Day 5

Deepen Understanding

Review Review word meanings for all oral vocabulary words. Use the definitions and examples from Day 1 and Day 3.

Guide Partner Activities Have partners work together to complete each of the activities below. Circulate and listen to partners as they work. Provide corrective feedback.

Examples Make a list of things that are so **tough** that they don't easily break or tear.

Describe Work with a partner. Take turns thinking of something in the classroom. Tell whether what you are thinking of is **shaped** like a circle, a square, a rectangle, or a triangle. Give other clues. Have your partner guess what you are thinking of.

Draw Draw a picture showing three things that are **different sizes**.

Role-Play Take turns acting out the following things with a partner. Show how you would **hop** over something. Show how you would **pull** something. Show how you would **reach** for something that is very high up. Show how you would walk to different parts of the room by **turning** one way or another. Then **come** back to where you started.

Compare Compare a kitten to a cat. Which one is **weaker**? Which one is older? Which one is bigger?

Assess To assess what word meanings children have learned, copy and distribute the **Pretest/Posttest** on pages 134–135. Use page 83 to administer the test. Compare scores with Day 1 assessment.

Unit 5, Lesson 22 • **T45**

Unit 5

Lesson 23

Days 1 and 2
"From Ducklings to Ducks," Vol. 2, pp. 30–31

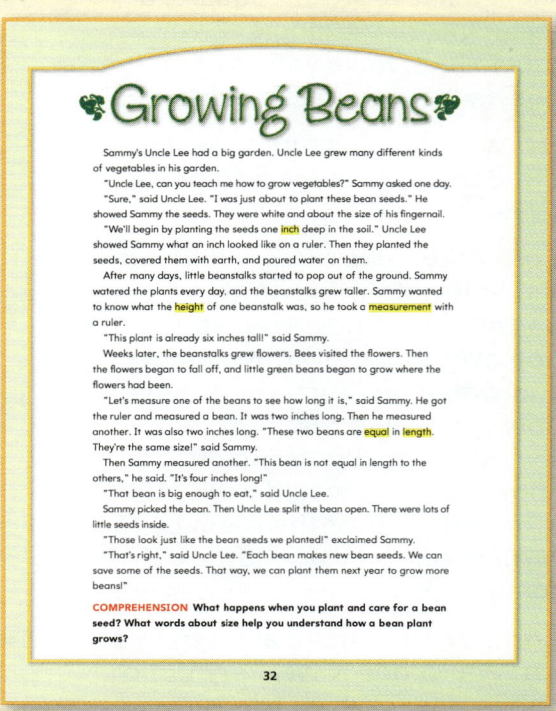

Days 3 and 4
"Growing Beans," Vol. 2, pp. 32–33

Assessment
Pretest/Posttest Administration p. 84

Pretest/Posttest Blackline Masters pp. 136–137

T46 • Curious About Words

Day 1

Introduce Meanings

Assess To assess what word meanings children already know, copy and distribute the **Pretest/Posttest** on pages 136–137. Use page 84 to administer the test.

Explain Write each oral vocabulary word below on the board. Read it aloud. Offer an explanation and a brief example for each word.

Words That Tell Where
down *adv.* from higher to lower *She climbed down the stairs.*
into *prep.* inside *I put the clothes into the box.*
off *adv.* no longer touching or on top of *Sam got off the swing and ran to the slide.*
out *adv.* no longer inside *The squirrel came out of a hole in the tree.*
outside *adv.* not inside *I went outside the store.*

Discuss Guide children to see the relationship between each word and the category. Take a pencil off of your desk. Ask, What did I just take **off** my desk? Put the pencil into a drawer. Ask, What did I just put the pencil **into**? Continue in the same way for the remaining words.

Read Aloud Explain that you will read aloud a story about how ducks grow. Then read aloud "From Ducklings to Ducks." Discuss the Comprehension questions.

Day 2

Categorize and Classify

Reread and Explain Reread "From Ducklings to Ducks." At the end of each sentence that includes an oral vocabulary word, stop and repeat the explanation of the word. Then reread the sentence.

Use a Graphic Organizer Use the graphic organizer and the questions below to reinforce understanding of the relationship between each word and the category.

```
        Moving Away
       From Something
         /    |    \
       off   out  outside
```

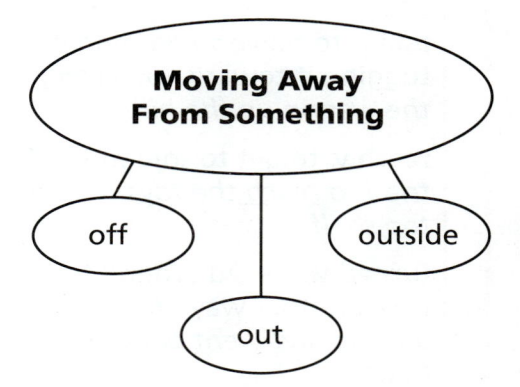

1. What might you see if you go **outside** your home? (Sample answers: trees; a yard; a sidewalk; a city street)

2. If you slid from the top to the bottom of a slide, which way did you go? (**down**)

3. Where do you put a key when you unlock a door? (**into** a lock)

15-20 Minute Lessons

Unit 5

Lesson 23

Day 3

Introduce Meanings

Explain Write each oral vocabulary word below on the board. Read it aloud. Offer an explanation and a brief example for each word.

Words About Size
equal *adj.* the same *Ben and I each have an equal number of cookies.*
height *n.* how tall something is *What is the height of this plant?*
inch *n.* a very small size used to tell how long something is *A peanut is about one inch long.*
length *n.* how long something is *The two pencils are the same length.*
measurement *n.* the size of something *You can use a ruler to take a measurement of your desk.*

Discuss Guide children to see the relationship between each word and the category. Have a few children line up in front of the class. Ask questions such as these: Are any children **equal** in **height**? Do any two children have legs that are equal **length**?

Read Aloud Explain that you will read aloud a story about a boy who helps out in his uncle's garden. Then read aloud "Growing Beans." Discuss the Comprehension questions.

Day 4

Categorize and Classify

Reread and Explain Reread "Growing Beans." At the end of each sentence that includes an oral vocabulary word, stop and repeat the explanation of the word. Then reread the sentence.

Use a Graphic Organizer Use the graphic organizer and the questions below to reinforce understanding of the relationship between each word and the category.

Words About Size	Words About Measurement
length height	inch equal

1. Name two things in the classroom that are about **equal** in **length**. (Sample answer: a pencil and a pair of scissors)
2. Which has greater **height**—a person or a house? (a house)
3. What is something you can use to take a **measurement** of how long something is? (Sample answer: a ruler)

Day 5

Deepen Understanding

Review Review word meanings for all oral vocabulary words. Use the definitions and examples from Day 1 and Day 3.

Guide Partner Activities Have partners work together to complete each of the activities below. Circulate and listen to partners as they work. Provide corrective feedback.

Compare Work with a partner. Compare the **length** of two things in your classroom. Which one is longer? What could you use to take a **measurement** and find out for sure?

Describe Pretend you went **into** the ocean and traveled **down** to the bottom of the sea. Describe to your partner what you might find there.

Examples Talk to your partner. Give examples of things you like to do when you go **outside** to play.

Draw Draw two flowers of **equal height**.

Role-Play Show how you might jump **out** of a hole in the ground. Show how you would pick up something only one **inch** long. Then show how you might take something **off** your desk and put it on the floor.

Assess To assess what word meanings children have learned, copy and distribute the **Pretest/Posttest** on pages 136–137. Use page 84 to administer the test. Compare scores with Day 1 assessment.

Unit 5, Lesson 23 • **T47**

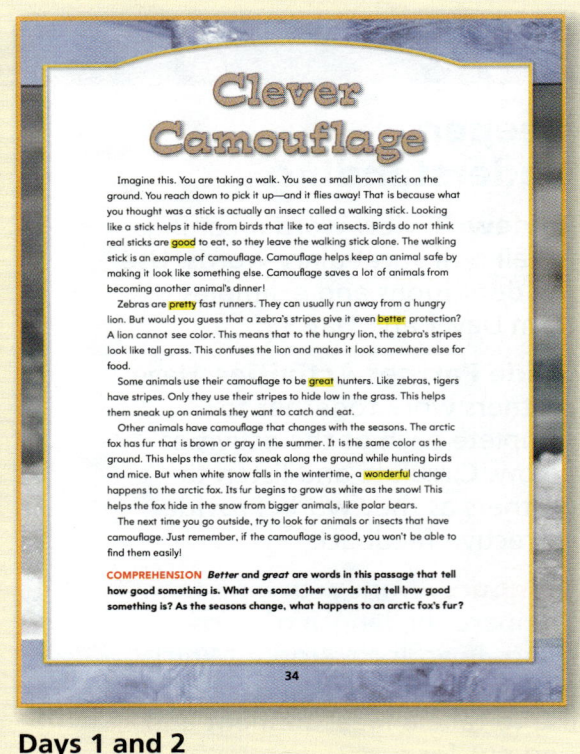

Unit 5
Lesson 24

Days 1 and 2

"Clever Camouflage," Vol. 2, pp. 34–35

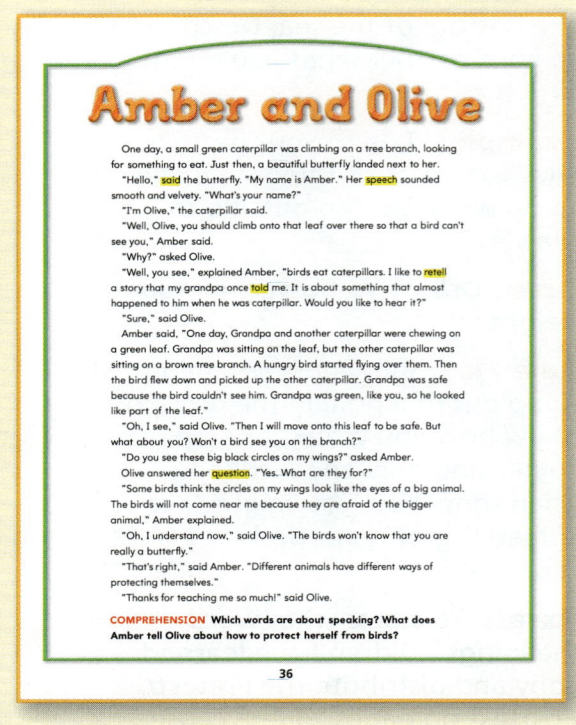

Days 3 and 4

"Amber and Olive," Vol. 2, pp. 36–37

Assessment

Pretest/Posttest Administration p. 85

Pretest/Posttest Blackline Masters pp. 138–139

T48 • Curious About Words

Day 1

Introduce Meanings

Explain To assess what word meanings children already know, copy and distribute the **Pretest/Posttest** on pages 138–139. Use page 85 to administer the test.

Explain Write each oral vocabulary word below on the board. Read it aloud. Offer an explanation and a brief example for each word.

Words About How Good Something Is

better *adj.* more special or more useful than something else *This cake is better than the last one you made.*

good *adj.* something someone likes *He thought it was a good movie.*

great *adj.* better than good; the best *He is a great baseball player.*

pretty *adv.* very; really *The runners went pretty fast.*

wonderful *adj.* really great; amazing *The story about the hero was wonderful.*

Discuss Guide children to see the relationship between each word and the category. Ask questions such as these: What kind of food tastes **good**? What food tastes **better**? What tastes **wonderful**?

Read Aloud Explain that you will read aloud an article about how animals use camouflage, or a special kind of appearance, to hide themselves. Then read aloud "Clever Camouflage." Discuss the Comprehension questions.

Day 2

Categorize and Classify

Reread and Explain Reread "Clever Camouflage." At the end of each sentence that includes an oral vocabulary word, stop and repeat the explanation of the word. Then reread the sentence.

Use a Graphic Organizer Use the graphic organizer and the questions below to reinforce understanding of the relationship between each word and the category.

```
         Words for
      Comparing Things
       /      |      \
    good   better   great
```

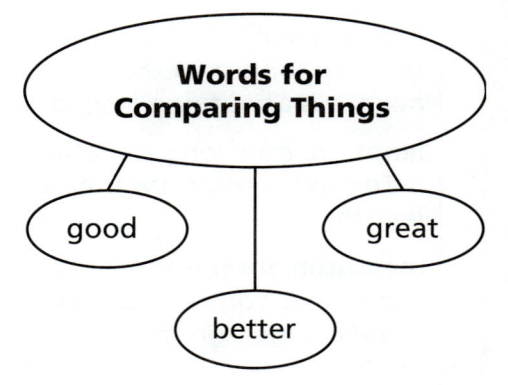

1. I am a fast runner, but Ayumi is really fast. She is _____. (**better**)
2. Would you rather have a meal that is **good** or **wonderful**? (**wonderful**)
3. Jimmy gets an A on every test. He is _____. (**great**)
4. Name two things you think are **pretty** good. (Answers will vary.)

15-20 Minute Lessons

Unit 5

Lesson 24

Day 3

Introduce Meanings

Explain Write each oral vocabulary word below on the board. Read it aloud. Offer an explanation and a brief example for each word.

Words About Speaking

question *n.* something you ask when you want to find out about something *May I ask you a question?*

retell *v.* to tell again *Mom likes to retell a story she heard as a young girl.*

said *v.* spoken *We listened carefully to what Dad said.*

speech *n.* the way one talks *The girl's speech sounded loud in the small room.*

told *v.* spoke about *My teacher told us how a caterpillar changes into a butterfly.*

Discuss Guide children to see the relationship between each word and the category. Use prompts and questions such as these: What is something important that someone in your family **told** you? **Retell** what he or she **said**.

Read Aloud Explain that you will read aloud a story about butterflies and caterpillars using camouflage. Then read aloud "Amber and Olive." Discuss the Comprehension questions.

Day 4

Categorize and Classify

Read and Explain Reread "Amber and Olive." At the end of each sentence that includes an oral vocabulary word, stop and repeat the explanation of the word. Then reread the sentence.

Use a Graphic Organizer Use the graphic organizer and the questions below to reinforce understanding of the relationship between each word and the category.

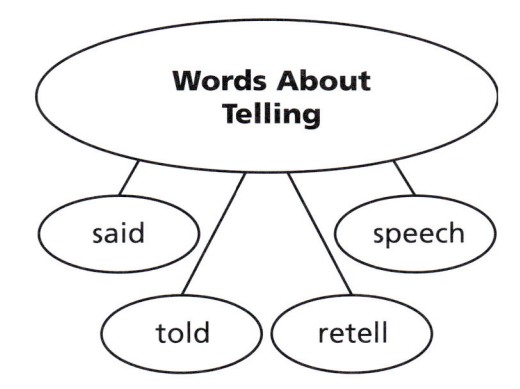

Words About Telling
- said
- speech
- told
- retell

1. Juan **told** us a story that his grandmother had told him. What did Juan do? **(retell)**

2. If someone told you a fact and you wanted to know more, what could you do? **(ask a question)**

Day 5

Review Repeat explanations for all oral vocabulary words. Use the definitions and examples from Day 1 and Day 3.

Guide Partner Activities Have partners work together to complete each of the activities below. Circulate and listen to partners as they work. Provide corrective feedback.

Categorize Work with a partner. Ask your partner **questions** about what foods he or she enjoys most. Name three foods that you think are **good** to eat.

Role-Play **Retell** a story you have heard. Tell what happened in the beginning, middle, and end.

Examples Give examples of things your teacher **told** you or **said** to your class.

Describe Talk to your partner. Use careful **speech** to describe something **wonderful**. Then describe something that goes **pretty** fast.

Draw Draw pictures of two things, and then choose the picture you think is **better** than the other. List reasons why the picture you like better is **great**.

Assess To assess what word meanings children have learned, copy and distribute the **Pretest/Posttest** on pages 138–139. Use page 85 to administer the test. Compare scores with Day 1 assessment.

Unit 5, Lesson 24 • **T49**

Unit 5
Lesson 25

Popcorn from Scratch

Did you know that popcorn doesn't have to come from a microwave? You can grow and **make** your own popcorn at home! Here's how.

Popcorn comes from a corn plant. If you **want** to grow your own popcorn, you first need to plant the corn seeds in the ground. But you can't **use** any kind of corn seeds to grow popcorn. You will need to use special popcorn seeds. Also, you can't use any dirt in your backyard. Ask a grownup to help you find the right kind of dirt to plant in.

Plant the popcorn seeds in early spring. Make a hole in the ground for each seed. **Try** to make each hole one to two inches deep. Ask a grownup to measure each hole with a ruler. Then fill in the holes with dirt.

After you plant your seeds, give them lots of water. You will need to water them **again** every few days. Soon the corn plants will start to grow.

The plants will grow taller and taller. Each plant will grow a few ears of corn. Each ear will have many seeds. These seeds are called kernels. After about four months, the plants will stop growing. Then you can pick the ears of corn. You pull them right off the plant.

After you pick the ears of corn, leave them in a safe, dry place for two weeks. When the corn feels hard and dry, you can pull the small, round kernels, or seeds, off the cob. Now it's time for you and a grownup to make popcorn!

Get a pot with a lid. Then pour a little vegetable oil into the pot. Put in a few handfuls of popcorn kernels, but don't fill up the pot! The kernels need lots of room to pop. Put the lid on the pot, and then put the pot on the stove. Use medium heat to cook the popcorn. In a few minutes, you will hear the corn start to pop. When the popping sound stops, take the pot off the stove. Open it up, and enjoy your snack!

COMPREHENSION Describe the steps for growing and making popcorn. What words about trying help you understand the kind of work it takes to grow and make popcorn?

38

Days 1 and 2

"Popcorn from Scratch," Vol. 2, pp. 38–39

A Harvest Feast

I woke up in the morning and quickly got dressed. It was the day of **our** family's harvest feast! Every fall, we visit my aunt and uncle's farm. There, we pick fruits and vegetables for our harvest feast.

When we arrived at the farm, my sister, Mary, and I raced to the garden. Aunt Jane was standing there. "Hi, Aunt Jane," we yelled. "We're here!"

"Hi there, girls," Aunt Jane said, smiling. "Let's get busy."

We picked tomatoes and cucumbers from **their** vines. We dug up potatoes and carrots. Then we picked lettuce leaves, squash, and peppers. After bringing the vegetables to the kitchen, we grabbed some baskets and headed to the blueberry bushes. We filled two huge baskets in no time. "What will we do with all of these blueberries, Aunt Jane?" I asked.

"Well," said Aunt Jane, "how does blueberry pie sound?"

"Great!" I said. "We love **your** blueberry pie!"

Then Aunt Jane said, "While I make the pie, why don't you two find Uncle Mark and pick some apples? Then we can make apple cider."

We ran out of the house and found Uncle Mark standing with Mom and Dad under the apple trees. "Hi, Uncle Mark," I said. "We're here to pick apples. Aunt Jane said we can make apple cider." We filled a cart with apples, and then Uncle Mark showed us how to make cider by using **his** apple press.

Later, it was time for our feast! Fresh fruits and vegetables make the most delicious meal! We had a stew with potatoes, carrots, and squash. We had a huge salad, too. And then, just when I thought I couldn't eat any more, Aunt Jane brought out dessert!

I'm already looking forward to next year's feast. Maybe someday I'll have my **own** farm!

COMPREHENSION Which words tell about things that belong to someone or something? What are some foods the family makes from freshly picked fruits and vegetables?

40

Days 3 and 4

"A Harvest Feast," Vol. 2, pp. 40–41

Assessment

Pretest/Posttest Administration p. 86

Pretest/Posttest Blackline Masters pp. 140–141

T50 • Curious About Words

Day 1

Introduce Meanings

Explain To assess what word meanings children already know, copy and distribute the **Pretest/Posttest** on pages 140–141. Use page 86 to administer the test.

Explain Write each oral vocabulary word below on the board. Read it aloud. Offer an explanation and a brief example for each word.

Words About Effort

again *adv.* another time *I can help you <u>again</u> tomorrow.*

make *v.* to create something *I will <u>make</u> you dinner.*

try *v.* to make an effort to do something *Mom will <u>try</u> to leave work early.*

use *v.* to do something with something else *Fran will <u>use</u> a backpack to carry her books.*

want *v.* to wish to do or have something *The twins <u>want</u> to buy Mom a gift.*

Discuss Guide children to see the relationship between each word and the category. Ask: What is something you would like to **try** to do? Why do you **want** to do it?

Read Aloud Explain that you will read aloud a description about the effort it takes to make popcorn. Then read aloud "Popcorn from Scratch." Discuss the Comprehension questions.

Day 2

Categorize and Classify

Reread and Explain Reread "Popcorn from Scratch." At the end of each sentence that includes an oral vocabulary word, stop and repeat the explanation of the word. Then reread the sentence.

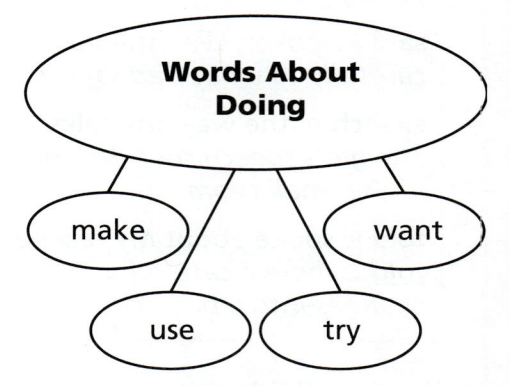

Use a Graphic Organizer Use the graphic organizer and the questions below to reinforce understanding of the relationship between each word and the category.

```
        Words About
           Doing
       /    |    \
    make   want
      \   /
     use  try
```

1. What might you **use** to **make** popcorn? (Sample answer: corn kernels, vegetable oil, a pot, a stove)

2. What kind of person do you **want** to be? (Sample answers: kind; friendly; helpful; happy)

3. If you **try** to do something and are unable to do it, you should try _____. (**again**)

15-20 Minute Lessons

Unit 5

Lesson 25

Day 3

Introduce Meanings

Explain Write each oral vocabulary word below on the board. Read it aloud. Offer an explanation and a brief example for each word.

Words About What Is Yours

his *pron.* belonging to a boy or man *The boy shared his fruit with a friend.*

our *adj.* belonging to us *Our school is having a book fair.*

own *adj.* mine; belonging only to me *I would like to have my own room instead of sharing with my sisters.*

their *adj.* belonging to other people *Their garden has beautiful flowers.*

your *adj.* belonging to you *Your dog likes to run and jump.*

Discuss Guide children to see the relationship between each word and the category. Ask: What words would you use to show that something is **owned** only by you? What words would you use to show that something is someone else's?

Read Aloud Explain that you will read aloud a story about how everyone who belongs to a family contributes to a feast. Then read aloud "A Harvest Feast." Discuss the Comprehension questions.

Day 4

Categorize and Classify

Read and Explain Reread "A Harvest Feast." At the end of each sentence that includes an oral vocabulary word, stop and repeat the explanation of the word. Then reread the sentence.

Use a Graphic Organizer Use the graphic organizer and the questions below to reinforce understanding of the relationship between each word and the category.

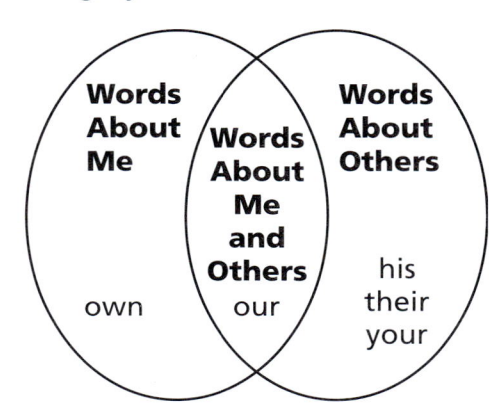

Words About Me: own
Words About Me and Others: our
Words About Others: his, their, your

1. What word tells that something belongs to you? (**your**)
2. If you and a friend had a farm, what word would you use to show it belonged to both of you? (**our**)
3. Why might you want **your own** garden? (Sample answer: I could grow the vegetables that I like best.)

Day 5

Deepen Understanding

Review Repeat explanations for all oral vocabulary words. Use the definitions and examples from Day 1 and Day 3.

Guide Partner Activities Have partners work together to complete each of the activities below. Circulate and listen to partners as they work. Provide corrective feedback.

Categorize Sort this list into things you can **make** and things you can **use**: rake, cake, painting, bike, pan, snowman.

Examples With a partner, come up with examples of things you have done that you would like to do **again**.

Describe Try to describe to a partner what **your own** room looks like. Use the words "My room is..." Then work together to describe **our** classroom.

Draw Draw and label a picture of what you **want** to do when you grow up.

Compare Think about what your family most often eats for dinner. Compare the food your family eats with the food your partner's family eats. How is your family's food similar to **their** food? Use the words "**His** family..." or "Her family..." as you compare.

Assess To assess what word meanings children have learned, copy and distribute the **Pretest/Posttest** on pages 140–141. Use page 86 to administer the test. Compare scores with Day 1 assessment.

Unit 5, Lesson 25 • **T51**

Unit 6
Lesson 26

Maggie's Big Day

Days 1 and 2
"Maggie's Big Day," Vol. 2, pp. 42–43

A Time to Help

Days 3 and 4
"A Time to Help," Vol. 2, pp. 44–45

Assessment

Pretest/Posttest Administration p. 87

Pretest/Posttest Blackline Masters pp. 142–143

T52 • Curious About Words

Day 1

Introduce Meanings

Assess To assess what word meanings children already know, copy and distribute the **Pretest/Posttest** on pages 142–143. Use page 87 to administer the test.

Explain Write each oral vocabulary word below on the board. Read it aloud. Offer an explanation and a brief example for each word.

Words About Shopping

buy *v.* to pay money to get something *Mom will buy me a book and crayons.*

money *n.* coins and bills used to pay for something *I have enough money to buy a game.*

open *v.* to make something not closed *Please open the door and come inside.*

sell *v.* to give something when someone pays you money *I will sell you my bike for fifty dollars.*

spend *v.* to pay money *I can spend five dollars on a birthday gift for my friend.*

Discuss Guide children to see the relationship between each word and the category. Prompt them to use the words to tell about a recent shopping trip.

Read Aloud Explain that you will read aloud a story about a girl who helps her dad at the family's grocery store. Then read aloud "Maggie's Big Day." Discuss the Comprehension questions.

Day 2

Categorize and Classify

Reread and Explain Reread "Maggie's Big Day." At the end of each sentence that includes an oral vocabulary word, stop and repeat the explanation of the word. Then reread the sentence.

Use a Graphic Organizer Use the graphic organizer and the questions below to reinforce understanding of the relationship between each word and the category.

Words About Getting: buy, spend
Both: money
Words About Giving: sell

1. What are some things that you can **open**? (Sample answer: a door, a window, a can of soup, a package, a letter, a store)

2. The word **buy** is the opposite of the word _____. (sell)

3. The word **spend** means almost the same as _____. (buy)

4. What does your family spend **money** on? (Sample answer: food, clothes, toys, gas)

15-20 Minute Lessons

Unit 6

Lesson 26

Day 3

Introduce Meanings

Explain Write each oral vocabulary word below on the board. Read it aloud. Offer an explanation and a brief example for each word.

Words About Other Names for People

he *pron.* a boy or a man *Steve works hard. He builds houses.*

I *pron.* me *My name is Nan. I like school.*

they *pron.* two or more other people *Mom and Dad are at home. They are working in the yard.*

we *pron.* me and at least one other person *Ted and I play soccer. We have games on Saturdays.*

you *pron.* how someone names me when they are talking to me *Lana asked a friend, "Do you want to ride bikes?"*

Discuss Guide children to see the relationship between each word and the category. Prompt them to use the words to talk about what they did last weekend and with whom.

Read Aloud Explain that you will read aloud a selection about children who help out after Hurricane Katrina. Then read aloud "A Time to Help." Discuss the Comprehension questions.

Day 4

Categorize and Classify

Reread and Explain Reread "A Time to Help." At the end of each sentence that includes an oral vocabulary word, stop and repeat the explanation of the word. Then reread the sentence.

Use a Graphic Organizer Use the graphic organizer and the questions below to reinforce understanding of the relationship between each word and the category.

Names for One Person	Names for Two or More People
I he you	we they you

1. What can **you** call yourself when you don't use your name? (**I**)
2. What word do you use to speak about one boy? (**he**)
3. If you used the word **we** in a sentence, whom might you be talking about? (Sample answers: Karen and I; my friends and I)

Day 5

Deepen Understanding

Review Repeat explanations for all oral vocabulary words. Use the definitions and examples from Day 1 and Day 3.

Guide Partner Activities Have partners work together to complete each of the activities below. Circulate and listen to partners as they work. Provide corrective feedback.

Categorize List three things that you would like to **buy**. List three things that you could **sell**.

Describe Talk to your partner. Imagine that your doorbell at home is ringing. Describe what happens when a family member **opens** the door. Who is there? Why did **he** or she come?

Draw Draw pictures of things you could **spend money** on in a toy store or in a bookstore.

Discuss Copy this sentence: **I** can _____. Talk to your partner about things that **you** can do.

Compare Talk to your partner. Use the words **they** and **we** in sentences. How are these words different? How are they the same?

Assess To assess what word meanings children have learned, copy and distribute the **Pretest/Posttest** on pages 142–143. Use page 87 to administer the test. Compare scores with Day 1 assessment.

Unit 6, Lesson 26 • **T53**

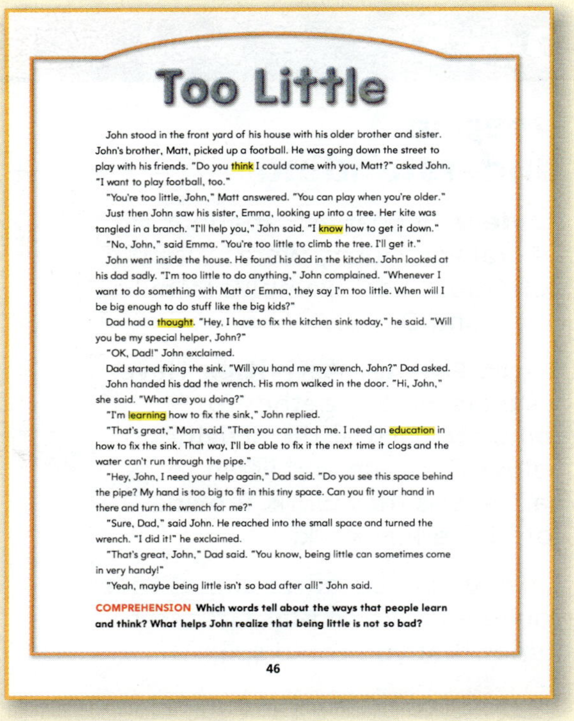

Unit 6
Lesson 27

"Too Little," Vol. 2, pp. 46–47
Days 1 and 2

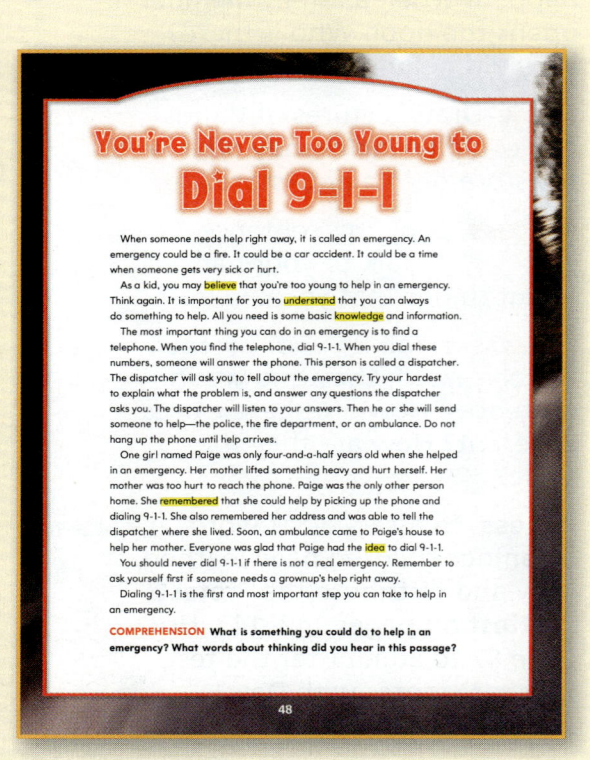

"You're Never Too Young to Dial 9-1-1," Vol. 2, pp. 48–49
Days 3 and 4

Assessment
Pretest/Posttest Administration p. 88
Pretest/Posttest Blackline Masters pp. 144–145

T54 • Curious About Words

Day 1

Introduce Meanings

Assess To assess what word meanings children already know, copy and distribute the **Pretest/Posttest** on pages 144–145. Use page 88 to administer the test.

Explain Write each oral vocabulary word below on the board. Read it aloud. Offer an explanation and a brief example for each word.

Words About Learning

education *n.* what you have when someone teaches you *I will get a good education if I pay attention in class and do all my work.*

know *v.* to understand *I know how to ride a bike because I learned last year.*

learning *v.* understanding and using what someone teaches you *The boys and girls in my class are learning how to read.*

think *v.* to have an idea or picture in your mind *I like to think about driving race cars.*

thought *n.* an idea *Dad had a thought about what to cook for dinner.*

Discuss Guide children to see the relationship between each word and the category. Ask them to talk about something they are **learning** in school. Prompt them to use each of the words.

Read Aloud Explain that you will read aloud a story about how the youngest child in a family learns to do something that helps his dad. Then read aloud "Too Little." Discuss the Comprehension questions.

Day 2

Categorize and Classify

Reread and Explain Reread "Too Little." At the end of each sentence that includes an oral vocabulary word, stop and repeat the explanation of the word. Then reread the sentence.

Use a Graphic Organizer Use the graphic organizer and the questions below to reinforce understanding of the relationship between each word and the category.

Words About Ideas
- think
- learning
- thought
- know

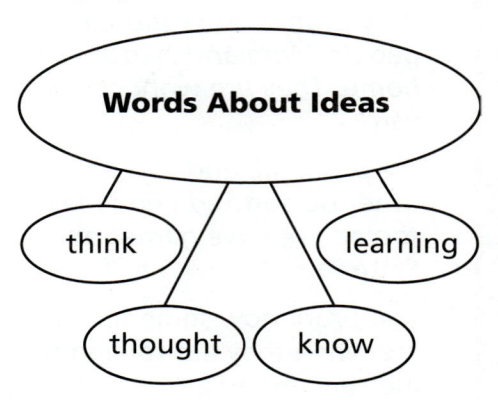

1. What are some things you are **learning** to do now? (Sample answer: read, swim, ride a bike)

2. Some people teach what they **know** to other people. They are giving these people an _____. (**education**)

3. What is something that you like to **think** about? (Answers will vary.)

Unit 6

Lesson 27

15-20 Minute Lessons

Day 3

Introduce Meanings

Explain Write each oral vocabulary word below on the board. Read it aloud. Offer an explanation and a brief example for each word.

Words About Thoughts and Thinking

believe *v.* to think something is true *I believe that my mom makes the best cake in the world.*

idea *n.* a thought *Jon has a great idea for his school project.*

knowledge *n.* information *My teacher has a lot of knowledge about animals because she owns four of them.*

remembered *v.* thought of again; did not forget *Sam remembered where he left his hat.*

understand *v.* to know what something means *I understand the directions for playing this game.*

Discuss Guide children to see the relationship between each word and the category. Ask: Which of these words helps tell about school? Explain your answers.

Read Aloud Explain that you will read aloud a selection about how calling 9-1-1 in an emergency is a good way to help. Then read aloud "You're Never Too Young to Dial 9-1-1." Discuss the Comprehension questions.

Day 4

Categorize and Classify

Reread and Explain Reread "You're Never Too Young to Dial 9-1-1." At the end of each sentence that includes an oral vocabulary word, stop and repeat the explanation of the word. Then reread the sentence.

Use a Graphic Organizer Use the graphic organizer and the questions below to reinforce understanding of the relationship between each word and the category.

Words About Thinking	Words About Thoughts
believe remembered understand	idea knowledge

1. What do you do to show that you **understand** what someone tells you? (Sample answer: repeat it back to the person)
2. What word might you use to describe something that happened yesterday? (**remembered**)
3. Suppose you were asked to think of an **idea** for a costume party. What would you say? (Answers will vary.)

Day 5

Deepen Understanding

Review Repeat explanations for all oral vocabulary words. Use the definitions and examples from Day 1 and Day 3.

Guide Partner Activities Have partners work together to complete each of the activities below. Circulate and listen to partners as they work. Provide corrective feedback.

Examples Give examples of things that you **believe** you are big enough to do. Explain to a partner why you are not too little to do these things.

Describe What do you know now that you did not know when you started kindergarten? Describe what you learned to your partner. Use the following words: **education, knowledge, remembered, think, thought.**

Discuss Tell your partner about some **ideas** you have about what you will learn in first grade. What will you **know** at the end of that year?

Role-Play Demonstrate for a partner some things you are **learning** to do at home. Then ask your partner to show that he or she **understands** what you are demonstrating.

Assess To assess what word meanings children have learned, copy and distribute the **Pretest/Posttest** on pages 144–145. Use page 88 to administer the test. Compare scores with Day 1 assessment.

Unit 6, Lesson 27 • **T55**

Unit 6
Lesson 28

Days 1 and 2
"The Art Contest," Vol. 2, pp. 50–51

Days 3 and 4
"Walt Disney," Vol. 2, pp. 52–53

Assessment
Pretest/Posttest Administration p. 89

Pretest/Posttest Blackline Masters pp. 146–147

T56 • Curious About Words

Day 1

Introduce Meanings

Assess To assess what word meanings children already know, copy and distribute the **Pretest/Posttest** on pages 146–147. Use page 89 to administer the test.

Explain Write each oral vocabulary word below on the board. Read it aloud. Offer an explanation and a brief example for each word.

Words About Art

draw *v.* to make a picture *Pamela likes to draw dinosaurs with her crayons.*

hang *v.* to attach something so it is held from above *My dad likes to hang my pictures on the wall.*

paint *v.* to use a brush to make a picture with colors *Elena used six colors to paint a rainbow.*

pictures *n.* drawings or paintings *Mike drew pictures of his house, his family, his dog, and his bike.*

show *v.* to let people see what you have or did *Please show me what you colored.*

Discuss Guide children to see the relationship between each word and the category. Ask volunteers to point to drawings, paintings, or **pictures** in the room.

Read Aloud Explain that you will read aloud a story about a mouse who gets the courage to join the school art contest. Then read aloud "The Art Contest." Discuss the Comprehension questions.

Day 2

Categorize and Classify

Reread and Explain Reread "The Art Contest." At the end of each sentence that includes an oral vocabulary word, stop and repeat the explanation of the word. Then reread the sentence.

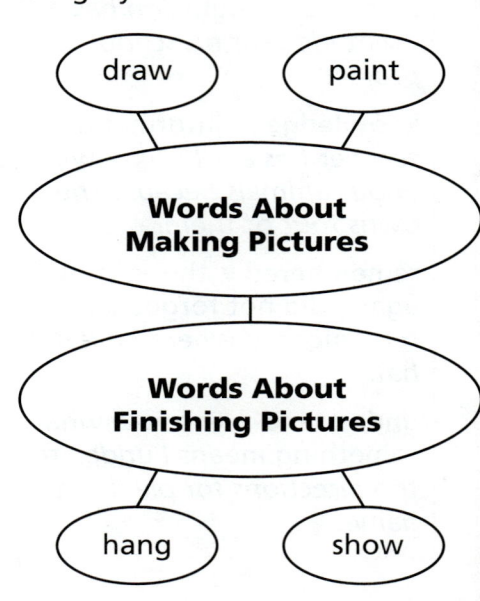

Use a Graphic Organizer Use the graphic organizer and the questions below to reinforce understanding of the relationship between each word and the category.

```
   (draw)        (paint)
       \         /
    (Words About
    Making Pictures)
           |
    (Words About
   Finishing Pictures)
       /         \
   (hang)        (show)
```

1. What kind of **pictures** do you like to **draw**? (Sample answer: flowers, animals)

2. If everyone in your class **painted** a picture, what might your teacher do with them? (Sample answers: **hang** them in the classroom; **show** them to our families)

Unit 6

Lesson 28

15-20 Minute Lessons

Day 3

Introduce Meanings

Explain Write each oral vocabulary word below on the board. Read it aloud. Offer an explanation and a brief example for each word.

Words About Places

California *n.* a state in the United States *Last year, my family moved to California.*

city *n.* a busy place where many people live and work *The city is an exciting place full of fun things to see and do.*

museum *n.* a building where people show art *I got to see many beautiful paintings at the museum.*

school *n.* a place where people teach and learn *Sue is learning to read at school.*

station *n.* a place where people get on or off buses or trains *Dad got to the station in time to get on his train.*

Discuss Guide children to see the relationship between each word and the category. Ask them to name which of these places they have been to.

Read Aloud Explain that you will read aloud a story about Walt Disney and some places that were special to him. Then read aloud "Walt Disney." Discuss the Comprehension questions.

Day 4

Categorize and Classify

Reread and Explain Reread "Walt Disney." At the end of each sentence that includes an oral vocabulary word, stop and repeat the explanation of the word. Then reread the sentence.

Use a Graphic Organizer Use the graphic organizer and the questions below to reinforce understanding of the relationship between each word and the category.

Words About Places to Live	Words About Places to Learn
city California	school museum

1. We bought a ticket for the bus at the _____. (**station**)

2. What kind of **museum** would you like to go to? (Sample answers: sports museum; science museum)

3. If you went to art **school**, what might you do? (Sample answers: draw; paint; work with clay)

Day 5

Deepen Understanding

Review Repeat explanations for all oral vocabulary words. Use the definitions and examples from Day 1 and Day 3.

Guide Partner Activities Have partners work together to complete each of the activities below. Circulate and listen to partners as they work. Provide corrective feedback.

Categorize Work with a partner. List three things you could **show** someone how to do. Then list two things you might **hang** on a wall.

Examples California is one of the fifty states in the United States. With a partner, name other states you know.

Describe Talk to your partner. Describe a **city**. What would you see and hear there? What might you do in a city?

Draw Paint or **draw** a **picture**. Show it to a partner. Ask your partner to describe it.

Role-Play Show what you might do at these kinds of **stations**: a train station and a bus station. What might you find at a fire station?

Compare Talk to your partner. Discuss the ways a **school** and a **museum** are different. Then discuss how they are alike.

Assess To assess what word meanings children have learned, copy and distribute the **Pretest/Posttest** on pages 146–147. Use page 89 to administer the test. Compare scores with Day 1 assessment.

Unit 6, Lesson 28 • **T57**

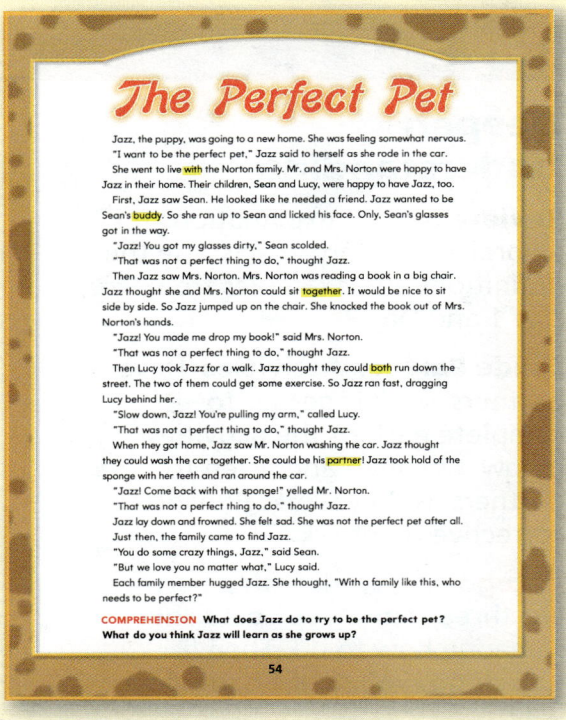

Unit 6
Lesson 29

The Perfect Pet

Days 1 and 2
"The Perfect Pet," Vol. 2, pp. 54–55

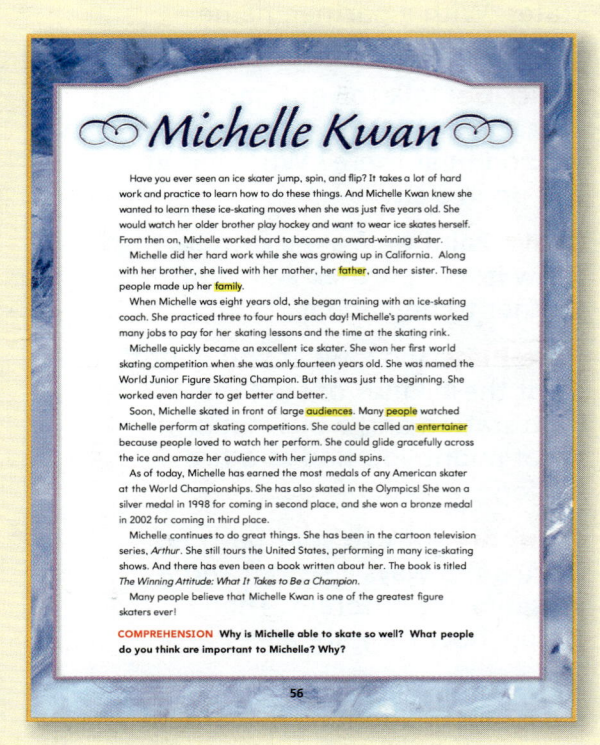

Michelle Kwan

Days 3 and 4
"Michelle Kwan," Vol. 2, pp. 56–57

Assessment
Pretest/Posttest Administration p. 90

Pretest/Posttest Blackline Masters
pp. 148–149

T58 • Curious About Words

Day 1

Introduce Meanings

Assess To assess what word meanings children already know, copy and distribute the **Pretest/Posttest** on pages 148–149. Use page 90 to administer the test.

Explain Write each oral vocabulary word below on the board. Read it aloud. Offer an explanation and a brief example for each word.

Words About Friends

both *pron.* two together *Both of us like chocolate ice cream.*

buddy *n.* a special friend *Cal is my buddy; we play together almost every day.*

partner *n.* a person who does something with you *Each child in my class had a partner to work with on the art project.*

together *adv.* with each other *Mom and I will go together to give the cake to our new neighbor.*

with *prep.* going together or being together *I went to the movies with my friends.*

Discuss Guide children to see the relationship between each word and the category. Ask: Who can tell me about a time when you played **together with** a **buddy**? Prompt children to use the other words.

Read Aloud Explain that you will read aloud a story about how a puppy tried to find ways to get others in the family to like her. Then read aloud "The Perfect Pet." Discuss the Comprehension questions.

Day 2

Categorize and Classify

Reread and Explain Reread "The Perfect Pet." At the end of each sentence that includes an oral vocabulary word, stop and repeat the explanation of the word. Then reread the sentence.

Use a Graphic Organizer Use the graphic organizer and the questions below to reinforce understanding of the relationship between each word and the category.

```
         Words to Tell About Friends
        /        |        |        \
     buddy   together  partner   with
                    \    /
                    both
```

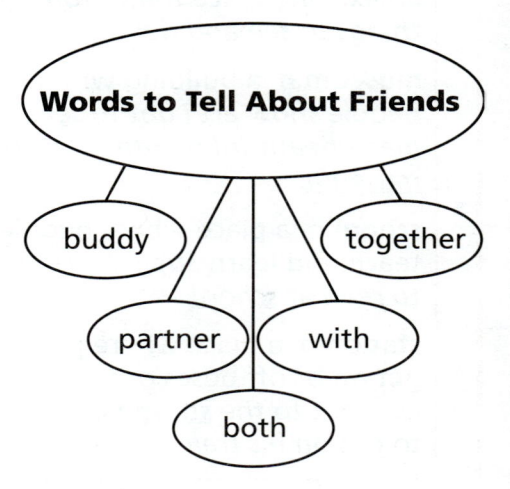

1. How do you know someone is your **buddy**? (Sample answer: He or she likes to play with me; we share.)

2. What do **both** you and a friend like to do **together**? (Answers will vary.)

3. What do you like to do **with** your mom or dad? (Answers will vary.)

4. When you go on a field trip at school, you might have a _____. (partner)

15-20 Minute Lessons

Unit 6

Lesson 29

Day 3

Introduce Meanings

Explain Write each oral vocabulary word below on the board. Read it aloud. Offer an explanation and a brief example for each word.

Words About People

audience *n.* people who get together to see or hear something *When the band finished playing, the <u>audience</u> clapped.*

entertainer *n.* a person who does something for other people to enjoy *The <u>entertainer</u> both sings and tells jokes.*

family *n.* parents and their children *My <u>family</u> likes to have pizza for dinner.*

father *n.* a man who has children *Dan's <u>father</u> coaches our soccer team.*

people *n.* men, women, boys, and girls *<u>People</u> go to a grocery store to buy food.*

Discuss Guide children to see the relationship between each word and the category. Use prompts such as these: Name an **entertainer** you enjoy. It could be an actor, a musician, or someone else. Tell about a time when you were in an **audience**. Name the **people** in your **family**.

Read Aloud Explain that you will read aloud a story about a skater named Michelle Kwan and the important people in her life. Then read aloud "Michelle Kwan." Discuss the Comprehension questions.

Day 4

Categorize and Classify

Reread and Explain Reread "Michelle Kwan." At the end of each sentence that includes an oral vocabulary word, stop and repeat the explanation of the word. Then reread the sentence.

Use a Graphic Organizer Use the graphic organizer and the questions below to reinforce understanding of the relationship between each word and the category.

People at Home	People at a Show
family father	audience entertainer

1. What do you call the **people** who sit and watch an **entertainer**? (audience)
2. What word might you use to describe one of the people in a **family**? (father)
3. What are some jobs people in your town or city have? (Sample answer: firefighter, police officer, teacher, mail carrier, store owner)

Day 5

Deepen Understanding

Review Repeat explanations for all oral vocabulary words. Use the definitions and examples from Day 1 and Day 3.

Guide Partner Activities Have partners work together to complete each of the activities below. Circulate and listen to partners as they work. Provide corrective feedback.

Categorize Work with a partner. List three **people** in your **family**. List three kinds of **entertainers**. Could a **father** be in both groups of people?

Draw Draw a picture of you playing at home **with** a **buddy**. Then tell your partner about your picture.

Examples Tell about another time when you did something in school with a **partner**. Tell what you **both** did **together**.

Role-Play Pretend you are part of a circus **audience**. Act out what you might see and do.

Assess To assess what word meanings children have learned, copy and distribute the **Pretest/Posttest** on pages 148–149. Use page 90 to administer the test. Compare scores with Day 1 assessment.

Unit 6, Lesson 29 • **T59**

Unit 6
Lesson 30

The Last Day of School

Days 1 and 2

"The Last Day of School," Vol. 2, pp. 58–59

Kindergarten Talent Show

Days 3 and 4

"Kindergarten Talent Show," Vol. 2, pp. 60–61

Assessment

Pretest/Posttest Administration p. 91

Pretest/Posttest Blackline Masters pp. 150–151

T60 • Curious About Words

Day 1

Introduce Meanings

Assess To assess what word meanings children already know, copy and distribute the **Pretest/Posttest** on pages 150–151. Use page 91 to administer the test.

Explain Write each oral vocabulary word below on the board. Read it aloud. Offer an explanation and a brief example for each word.

Words About a Party

celebrate *v.* to have a party *She will celebrate at her friend's birthday party.*

party *n.* when people get together to have fun *Sue invited friends to her house for a party.*

photograph *n.* a picture made by a camera *I have a photograph of my family.*

surprised *adj.* how you feel when something you didn't know about suddenly happens *I was surprised when Mom said we were going to the circus.*

wrapped *adj.* covered by paper or cloth *Children brought wrapped presents to the birthday party.*

Discuss Guide children to see the relationship between each word and the category. Ask: Who can tell me about a time when someone celebrated a birthday? What happened at the party? Prompt children to use the other words.

Read Aloud Explain that you will read aloud a story about a party in a kindergarten class on the last day of school. Then read aloud "The Last Day of School." Discuss the Comprehension questions.

Day 2

Categorize and Classify

Reread and Explain Reread "The Last Day of School." At the end of each sentence that includes an oral vocabulary word, stop and repeat the explanation of the word. Then reread the sentence.

Use a Graphic Organizer Use the graphic organizer and the questions below to reinforce understanding of the relationship between each word and the category.

Party Words	
Words That Go with People	Words That Go with Things
surprised celebrate	wrapped photograph

1. Name three things people do to **celebrate** at a **party**. (Sample answer: eat, dance, laugh)

2. At a party, you use a camera to take a _____. (**photograph**)

3. You can't see what a present is when it is _____. (**wrapped**)

15-20 Minute Lessons

Unit 6

Lesson 30

Day 3

Introduce Meanings

Explain Write each oral vocabulary word below on the board. Read it aloud. Offer an explanation and a brief example for each word.

Words About Choices

choices *n.* different things you can do or have *You have many choices of what to do at our class activity centers.*

decide *v.* to make up your mind; to choose one thing to do or have *Did you decide to eat an apple or a peach?*

information *n.* what you need to know; facts *The information about the field trip is in the letter.*

judge *v.* to listen or look at in order to decide *My mom will judge how much food I need for lunch.*

or *conj.* a word that tells there is a choice *I will buy you a book, a puzzle, or crayons.*

Discuss Guide children to see the relationship between each word and the category. Ask questions such as these: What **choices** do we make in our classroom? What **information** do I give you? What do you **decide** to do?

Read Aloud Explain that you will read aloud a selection about how children made choices before a kindergarten talent show. Then read aloud "Kindergarten Talent Show." Discuss the Comprehension questions.

Day 4

Categorize and Classify

Reread and Explain Reread "Kindergarten Talent Show." At the end of each sentence that includes an oral vocabulary word, stop and repeat the explanation of the word. Then reread the sentence.

Use a Graphic Organizer Use the graphic organizer and the questions below to reinforce understanding of the relationship between each word and the category.

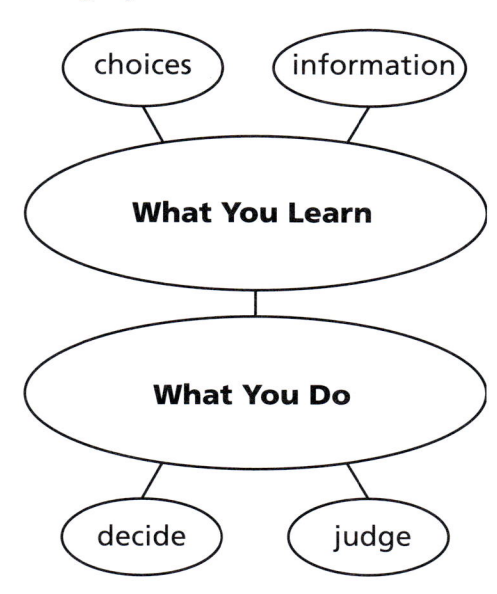

```
   choices        information
        \          /
         What You Learn
              |
         What You Do
         /          \
      decide       judge
```

1. What **information** do signs tell you? (Sample answer: stop, keep off, the name of a store, street names)

2. Would you rather play **or** watch a soccer game? (Answers will vary.)

3. If you help plan a dinner, what food would you **decide** to have? (Answers will vary.)

Day 5

Deepen Understanding

Review Repeat explanations for all oral vocabulary words. Use the definitions and examples from Day 1 and Day 3.

Guide Partner Activities Have partners work together to complete each of the activities below. Circulate and listen to partners as they work. Provide corrective feedback.

Categorize Work with a partner. List three things you could take a **photograph** of at a **party**.

Examples Give your partner two **choices** of something nice to have. Use the word **or** between the choices. Have your partner **decide** which choice to make. For example, do you want a rocket **or** an airplane?

Describe Talk to your partner. Describe a time you **celebrated** something special.

Draw Remember a time when your family members **surprised** you by giving you something they had **wrapped**. Draw a picture to show this and tell about it.

Write Tell your teacher your address and telephone number. Have her write this **information** on a card.

Discuss How do you **judge** what is the best kind of pet to own? Tell your partner about this pet. Explain why it is the best.

Assess To assess what word meanings children have learned, copy and distribute the **Pretest/Posttest** on pages 150–151. Use page 91 to administer the test. Compare scores with Day 1 assessment.

Unit 6, Lesson 30 • **T61**

Unit 1, Lesson 1

Pretest/Posttest Administration
Curious About Words

Grade K

Copy and distribute **Pretest/Posttest** pages 92–93. Also see directions, page 1.

Day 1–Day 2: Words About Moms

1. **her** Which picture shows someone with **her** pet?
   - ○ [boy with cat]
   - ○ [bird with worm]
   - ● [girl with cat]

2. **mother** Which picture shows a **mother**?
   - ○ [man and boy at pool]
   - ● [woman with children]
   - ○ [baby]

3. **parent** Which picture shows children with a **parent**?
   - ● [woman with kids at airport]
   - ○ [kids on slide]
   - ○ [girl with puppies]

4. **she** Which picture shows how **she** plays?
   - ○ [boy playing hopscotch]
   - ● [girl with hoop]
   - ○ [frog hopping]

Days 3–Day 4: Words About a Family Visit

5. **cousin** Which picture shows a girl and her **cousin**?
   - ● [girls]
   - ○ [girl beside taxi]
   - ○ [girl with horse]

6. **crowded** Which picture shows a **crowded** place?
   - ○ [boy at table]
   - ○ [empty park]
   - ● [amusement park]

7. **food** Which picture shows **food** you might see at a family party?
   - ● [snacks]
   - ○ [cats]
   - ○ [vehicles]

8. **visit** Which picture shows how people get ready to go **visit** their relatives?
   - ○ [man and woman at table]
   - ● [family packing van]
   - ○ [boy and man on couch]

Curious About Words
Copyright © Houghton Mifflin Harcourt Publishing Company

Pretest/Posttest Administration

Unit 1, Lesson 2

Pretest/Posttest Administration
Curious About Words
Grade K

Copy and distribute **Pretest/Posttest** pages 94–95. Also see directions, page 1.

Day 1–Day 2: Words About Being Safe in Water

1. **attention** Which picture shows someone who needs to pay **attention** to what he or she is doing?
   - ○ [boy sleeping]
   - ● [girl reading]
   - ○ [boy under tree]

2. **prevent** Which picture shows how to **prevent** pets from running away?
   - ● [2 rabbits in cage]
   - ○ [cat and dog going into house]
   - ○ [dog chasing cat]

3. **safety** Which picture shows the best example of bike **safety**?
   - ○ [boy straddling bike, ready to ride, without helmet]
   - ○ [girl on bike without helmet]
   - ● [boy on bike with helmet]

4. **water** Which picture shows children playing in **water**?
   - ● [swimming]
   - ○ [playing soccer]
   - ○ [girls swinging]

Day 3–Day 4: Words About Feelings

5. **curious** Which picture shows a child who might feel **curious**?
   - ● [girl with present]
   - ○ [child carrying a heavy box]
   - ○ [girl sleeping]

6. **furious** Which picture shows something that might make a dog's owner **furious**?
   - ○ [girl walking dog]
   - ● [dog chewing slipper]
   - ○ [dog in bed]

7. **impatient** Which picture shows a time when children might feel **impatient**?
   - ○ [children running in sprinkler]
   - ● [class at zoo]
   - ○ [2 kids with cat]

8. **shocked** Which picture shows something a parent might be **shocked** to see?
   - ○ [flowers on table]
   - ○ [picture in frame]
   - ● [broken picture]

Unit 1, Lesson 3

Grade K

Pretest/Posttest Administration
Curious About Words

Copy and distribute **Pretest/Posttest** pages 96–97. Also see directions, page 1.

Day 1–Day 2: Words About Size

1. **enormous** Which picture shows an **enormous** animal?
   - ○ [bird]
   - ○ [fish]
   - ● [elephant]
2. **large** Which picture shows a **large** plant?
   - ● [tree]
   - ○ [carrot]
   - ○ [pot of flowers]
3. **little** Which picture shows **little** toys?
   - ● [marbles]
   - ○ [blocks]
   - ○ [stuffed animals]
4. **small** Which picture shows a **small** animal?
   - ○ [whale]
   - ○ [tiger]
   - ● [frog]

Day 3–Day 4: Words About Time

5. **sometimes** Which picture shows something that children **sometimes** do at school?
   - ○ [girl skiing]
   - ● [boy painting at easel]
   - ○ [boy in bunk bed]
6. **soon** Which picture shows what might happen **soon** after you write a letter?
   - ● [girl putting letter in mailbox]
   - ○ [boy taking pencil out of box]
   - ○ [boy sharpening pencil]
7. **suddenly** Which picture shows something that might happen **suddenly** during the day?
   - ○ [vegetables ready to pick]
   - ● [raining]
   - ○ [spider spinning a web]
8. **until** Which picture shows children playing **until** one side wins?
   - ● [tug of war]
   - ○ [tea party]
   - ○ [girl flying a kite]

Unit 1, Lesson 4

Grade K

Pretest/Posttest Administration
Curious About Words

Copy and distribute **Pretest/Posttest** pages 98–99. Also see directions, page 1.

Day 1–Day 2: Words About Helping Out

1. **chores** Which picture shows a boy doing one of his **chores**?
   - ○ [boy kicking ball]
   - ● [boy feeding fish]
   - ○ [boy on slide]

2. **help** Which picture shows how a child can **help** at home?
   - ● [mom and boy in kitchen]
   - ○ [girl watching TV]
   - ○ [boy painting picture]

3. **responsibility** Which picture shows a **responsibility** people have for their pets?
   - ● [boy feeding cat]
   - ○ [dog and cat tugging on rope]
   - ○ [two girls looking at a cat]

4. **wash** Which picture shows something you would use to **wash** a floor?
   - ○ [rug]
   - ○ [rake]
   - ● [mop]

Day 3–Day 4: Words About Jobs

5. **busy** Which picture shows **busy** children?
   - ○ [children napping]
   - ○ [children at bus stop]
   - ● [children building house]

6. **job** Which picture shows something firefighters must have to do their **job**?
   - ○ [desk]
   - ○ [cap]
   - ● [fire truck]

7. **services** Which picture shows the **services** people enjoy when they eat at a restaurant?
   - ○ [a sink full of dishes]
   - ○ [teacher reading to children]
   - ● [waiter and person washing dishes]

8. **work** Which picture shows a person who is doing their **work**?
   - ○ [man waving]
   - ○ [boy with ice cream]
   - ● [boy raking leaves]

Unit 1, Lesson 5

Grade K

Pretest/Posttest Administration
Curious About Words

Copy and distribute **Pretest/Posttest** pages 100–101. Also see directions, page 1.

Day 1–Day 2: Words About Bugs

1. **gathered** Many bugs **gather** dirt to make a home. Which picture shows something that people have **gathered**?
   - ○ [owl in tree]
   - ● [fruits in a store]
   - ○ [tiger running]

2. **hill** A **hill** can be home to many kinds of bugs. Which picture shows a **hill**?
   - ○ [pond]
   - ○ [seashore]
   - ● [hill]

3. **tunnel** Some kinds of beetles make **tunnels** to live in. Which picture shows a **tunnel** that people would use?
   - ● [tunnel]
   - ○ [bridge]
   - ○ [road]

4. **worker** Finding food makes bugs hard **workers**. Which picture shows a **worker** who makes food for people?
   - ○ [boy eating]
   - ● [baker]
   - ○ [various food items]

Day 3–Day 4: Words About a Visit to the Doctor

5. **break** You would go to a doctor if you had a **break** in some part of your body. Which picture shows something that has a **break** in it?
   - ● [vase with crack]
   - ○ [glass]
   - ○ [table]

6. **healed** Which picture shows an animal with something that needs to be **healed**?
   - ○ [fox with wig]
   - ○ [cat with bone]
   - ● [rabbit with bandage]

7. **illness** Which picture shows an animal with an **illness**?
   - ● [sick lion]
   - ○ [cat eating]
   - ○ [pig with ribbon]

8. **injury** Which picture shows an animal with an **injury**?
   - ○ [rooster crowing]
   - ● [rabbit on crutches]
   - ○ [bee and flower]

Unit 2, Lesson 6

Grade K

Pretest/Posttest Administration
Curious About Words

Copy and distribute **Pretest/Posttest** pages 102–103. Also see directions, page 1.

Day 1–Day 2: Words About Sounds

1. **applause** Which picture shows **applause**?
   - ○ [boys looking at birds]
   - ● [man clapping for birthday cake]
   - ○ [band playing]

2. **bursting** Which picture shows something that could be **bursting** with a pop?
   - ○ [boy with piggy bank]
   - ○ [girl with envelope]
   - ● [boy with balloon]

3. **pounding** Which picture shows something that would make a **pounding** sound?
   - ○ [making a snowman]
   - ● [hammering nail]
   - ○ [eating fruit]

4. **screaming** Which picture shows an animal that might be **screaming** soon?
   - ● [lion pulling tooth]
   - ○ [rabbit drinking tea]
   - ○ [chick in bed]

Day 3–Day 4: Words About Our Senses

5. **noises** Which picture shows an animal that makes loud **noises**?
   - ● [dog]
   - ○ [turtle]
   - ○ [fish]

6. **scent** Which picture shows something that has a nice **scent**?
   - ○ [skunk]
   - ○ [pig in mud]
   - ● [flowers in pot]

7. **smooth** Which picture shows something that feels **smooth**?
   - ○ [rock]
   - ● [balloon]
   - ○ [caterpillar]

8. **vibration** Which picture shows something that makes a **vibration** you can feel?
   - ● [drum]
   - ○ [roll of tape]
   - ○ [book]

Unit 2, Lesson 7

Copy and distribute **Pretest/Posttest** pages 104–105. Also see directions, page 1.

Day 1–Day 2: Words About Sounds

1. **call** Which picture shows who or what might **call** someone?
   - ○ [sun]
   - ○ [stuffed animals]
   - ● [boy with pet dish]

2. **hear** Which picture shows something that people can **hear**?
   - ○ [cap]
   - ○ [bird's nest]
   - ● [children and a radio]

3. **sing** Which picture shows an animal that can **sing**?
   - ○ [goat]
   - ● [bird]
   - ○ [raccoon]

4. **sound** Which picture shows something that can make a **sound** all by itself?
   - ● [cat]
   - ○ [table]
   - ○ [lamp]

Day 3–Day 4: Words About Communication

5. **laughs** Which picture shows a child who **laughs**?
   - ○ [child with arms spread]
   - ● [boy with open mouth]
   - ○ [angry boy]

6. **message** Which picture shows things you can use to write a **message**?
   - ● [desk with paper and pencils]
   - ○ [coins on table]
   - ○ [games]

7. **talks** Which picture shows someone who **talks** a lot?
   - ● [woman in front of children]
   - ○ [girl with cookbook]
   - ○ [boy writing]

8. **voice** Which picture shows a place where people probably speak in a quiet **voice**?
   - ○ [fair]
   - ○ [playground]
   - ● [room inside a building]

Unit 2, Lesson 8

Copy and distribute **Pretest/Posttest** pages 106–107. Also see directions, page 1.

Grade K

Pretest/Posttest Administration

Curious About Words

Day 1–Day 2: Words About Moving Your Body

1. **bend** Which picture shows how a child can **bend**?
   - ○ [girl standing]
   - ● [boy watering seeds]
   - ○ [boy standing]

2. **motion** Which picture shows something that is a **motion**?
   - ● [girl jumping rope]
   - ○ [a cup]
   - ○ [a sandwich]

3. **muscles** Which picture shows something that can help build strong **muscles**?
   - ○ [soap]
   - ● [set of barbells]
   - ○ [eyeglasses]

4. **rest** Which picture shows a person who is taking a **rest**?
   - ● [man sitting on log]
   - ○ [girl on a bike]
   - ○ [boy in leaves]

Day 3–Day 4: Words About Animal Actions

5. **curled** Which picture shows something that has been **curled**?
   - ○ [pencil]
   - ○ [rug]
   - ● [water hose]

6. **escaping** Which picture shows one animal **escaping** from another?
   - ● [dog chasing cat up a tree]
   - ○ [dog and cat tug of war]
   - ○ [elephant and cat]

7. **race** Which picture shows people who are ready to **race**?
   - ○ [actors in a play]
   - ○ [boy dancing]
   - ● [people at a starting line]

8. **sneaked** Which picture shows what happened when a dog **sneaked** up somewhere?
   - ○ [boy giving dog treat]
   - ● [man scolding dog on chair]
   - ○ [boy with dog]

Unit 2, Lesson 9

Pretest/Posttest Administration
Curious About Words

Grade K

Copy and distribute **Pretest/Posttest** pages 108–109. Also see directions, page 1.

Day 1–Day 2: Words About Asking Questions

1. **how** Which picture shows **how** people play basketball?
   - ○ [basketball]
   - ● [basketball players]
   - ○ [basketball hoop]

2. **what** Which picture shows **what** you might take on a trip?
   - ○ [the zoo]
   - ● [map]
   - ○ [desk]

3. **where** Which picture shows a place **where** you can take a bath?
   - ○ [bed]
   - ● [bathtub]
   - ○ [soap]

4. **why** Which picture shows **why** a bike can't go?
   - ○ [bike]
   - ○ [girl riding bike]
   - ● [bike losing wheel]

Day 3–Day 4: Words About Building Things

5. **build** Which picture shows a person working to **build** something?
   - ○ [girl with dog]
   - ○ [woman playing golf]
   - ● [man and a wall]

6. **create** Which picture shows how a person can **create** something?
   - ○ [people looking at art]
   - ● [boy drawing]
   - ○ [someone putting on a shoe]

7. **shovels** Which picture shows a way to use **shovels**?
   - ● [man digging]
   - ○ [mom cooking]
   - ○ [boy sewing]

8. **tool** Which picture shows a **tool**?
   - ○ [yo-yo]
   - ○ [flower]
   - ● [hammer]

Unit 2, Lesson 10

Copy and distribute **Pretest/Posttest** pages 110–111. Also see directions, page 1.

Grade K

Pretest/Posttest Administration
Curious About Words

Day 1–Day 2: Words About What People Are Like

1. **character** Cinderella is a **character** in a story. Which picture shows a place where you might see other **characters**?
   - ○ [pet store]
   - ● [movie theater]
   - ○ [children on seesaw]

2. **funny** Which picture shows something **funny**?
   - ● [boy with birds on head]
   - ○ [girl cutting paper]
   - ○ [bag of groceries]

3. **kind** Which picture shows a way people can be **kind** to each other?
   - ○ [angry boys]
   - ○ [boys tugging coat]
   - ● [man helping girl]

4. **quiet** Which picture shows a **quiet** time?
   - ● [teacher reading]
   - ○ [children running race]
   - ○ [city scene]

Day 3–Day 4: Words That Tell Where

5. **around** Which picture shows something that is **around** the animals?
   - ○ [seals on rocks]
   - ○ [birds on feeder]
   - ● [sheep in pen]

6. **between** Which picture shows a child who is **between** other children?
   - ○ [two children]
   - ● [girls jumping rope]
   - ○ [children feeding fish]

7. **over** Which picture shows something you can see **over** your head?
   - ○ [pond]
   - ● [sun]
   - ○ [gate]

8. **under** Which picture shows something you can walk **under**?
   - ● [monkey bars]
   - ○ [bus]
   - ○ [door]

Unit 3, Lesson 11

Pretest/Posttest Administration
Curious About Words

Grade K

Copy and distribute **Pretest/Posttest** pages 112–113. Also see directions, page 1.

Day 1–Day 2: Words About Migration

1. **beaks** Which picture shows animals that have **beaks**?
   - ● [birds on wire]
   - ○ [cats]
   - ○ [fish in bowl]

2. **bird** Which picture shows a **bird**?
   - ○ [animal with four legs]
   - ● [animal with wings]
   - ○ [animal with six arms]

3. **distance** Which picture shows people who have a big **distance** between them?
   - ● [children on a slide]
   - ○ [children hugging]
   - ○ [woman and girl standing]

4. **fly** Which picture shows an animal that can **fly**?
   - ○ [pig]
   - ○ [goat]
   - ● [bee]

Day 3–Day 4: Words About Seasons

5. **blooming** Which picture shows something that is **blooming**?
   - ○ [nuts]
   - ● [flowers]
   - ○ [bare tree]

6. **cold** Which picture shows children who are **cold**?
   - ○ [boys playing in waves]
   - ● [children shivering]
   - ○ [children playing in sprinkler]

7. **grow** Which picture shows something that can **grow**?
   - ● [boy watering plant]
   - ○ [wagon]
   - ○ [pencil]

8. **temperature** Which picture shows something most people would want to do only if the **temperature** was high enough?
   - ● [go to the beach]
   - ○ [read a book]
   - ○ [write a letter]

Curious About Words
Copyright © Houghton Mifflin Harcourt Publishing Company

Pretest/Posttest Administration

Unit 3, Lesson 12

Copy and distribute **Pretest/Posttest** pages 114–115. Also see directions, page 1.

Grade K

Pretest/Posttest Administration
Curious About Words

Day 1–Day 2: Words About Storms

1. **damage** A storm can sometimes **damage** things outside. Which picture shows an animal that is going to **damage** something that is inside?
   - ○ [cat sleeping by fire]
   - ● [dog chewing slippers]
   - ○ [piggy bank with money]

2. **dangerous** It can be **dangerous** to walk outside in a storm. Which picture shows a place inside where it looks **dangerous** to walk?
   - ● [stairs with toys on them]
   - ○ [a gym]
   - ○ [a yard]

3. **shake** A big storm can **shake** a tree. Which picture shows something *you* can **shake**?
   - ○ [birthday cake]
   - ○ [ice-cream cone]
   - ● [bottle of juice]

4. **wind** A storm can bring a lot of **wind**. Which picture shows a toy that works best when there is a lot of **wind** without a storm?
   - ○ [top]
   - ○ [checkers]
   - ● [kite]

Day 3–Day 4: Words About School

5. **paper** Which picture shows a person working on a **paper**?
   - ○ [boy on floor]
   - ○ [man outside]
   - ● [person holding something]

6. **stories** Which picture shows something that has **stories**?
   - ● [book]
   - ○ [food in bag]
   - ○ [puzzle]

7. **teacher** Which picture shows a **teacher**?
   - ○ [person putting out a fire]
   - ● [person reading to children]
   - ○ [person selling a baseball glove]

8. **write** Which picture shows something you can use to **write** a story?
   - ● [pencil]
   - ○ [straw]
   - ○ [baseball bat]

Curious About Words
Copyright © Houghton Mifflin Harcourt Publishing Company

Pretest/Posttest Administration

Unit 3, Lesson 13

Grade K

Pretest/Posttest Administration
Curious About Words

Copy and distribute **Pretest/Posttest** pages 116–117. Also see directions, page 1.

Day 1–Day 2: Words About Colors

1. **blue** Which picture shows a food that could be **blue**?
   - ○ [pineapples]
   - ○ [bananas]
   - ● [berries]

2. **brown** Which picture shows food that is **brown**?
   - ● [walnut in its shell]
   - ○ [corn]
   - ○ [apple]

3. **green** Which picture shows an animal that is **green**?
   - ● [grasshopper]
   - ○ [hen]
   - ○ [fox]

4. **yellow** Which picture shows something that is **yellow**?
   - ○ [pig]
   - ● [sun]
   - ○ [log]

Day 3–Day 4: Words for Describing Animals

5. **colors** Some animals, such as bears, can be different **colors**. Which picture shows a kind of food that comes in different **colors**?
   - ● [grapes (red, green, purple)]
   - ○ [pineapple (yellow)]
   - ○ [carrot (orange)]

6. **eyes** Most animals have **eyes**. Which picture shows **eyes**?
   - ○ [things that help you touch]
   - ● [things that help you see]
   - ○ [something that helps you smell]

7. **head** Most animals have a **head**, just like people do. Which picture shows something you can put on your **head**?
   - ○ [shoes]
   - ○ [baseball glove]
   - ● [cap]

8. **trait** Different animals sometimes share the same **trait**. Think about the sun, an orange, and a balloon. Which picture shows a **trait** that all three of them share?
   - ● [round, like a circle]
   - ○ [yellow, like a banana]
   - ○ [in the sky, like a cloud]

Curious About Words
Copyright © Houghton Mifflin Harcourt Publishing Company

Pretest/Posttest Administration

Unit 3, Lesson 14

Pretest/Posttest Administration
Curious About Words
Grade K

Copy and distribute **Pretest/Posttest** pages 118–119. Also see directions, page 1.

Day 1–Day 2: Words About Distance

1. **area** Which picture shows an **area** for playing?
   - ○ [drum]
   - ● [playground]
   - ○ [tying a shoe]

2. **deepest** Which picture shows the person who is going the **deepest** of all the swimmers?
   - ○ [swimmers racing]
   - ○ [girl swimming]
   - ● [person diving under the water]

3. **far** Which picture shows something you can ride in to go **far** away?
   - ○ [wagon]
   - ● [plane]
   - ○ [skateboard]

4. **near** Which picture shows something it might be nice to be **near** on a hot day?
   - ● [the beach]
   - ○ [fireplace]
   - ○ [hot stove]

Day 3–Day 4: Words About Actions

5. **climbing** Which picture shows a person **climbing**?
   - ○ [boy on horse]
   - ● [girl moving up rock wall]
   - ○ [boy gymnast]

6. **eat** Which picture shows something you can use to **eat** with?
   - ○ [pen]
   - ● [spoon]
   - ○ [toothbrush]

7. **landing** Which picture shows someone **landing** in the water?
   - ● [girl jumping]
   - ○ [swimmers]
   - ○ [girl on board]

8. **live** Which picture shows a place where people can **live**?
   - ○ [nest]
   - ○ [log]
   - ● [house]

Curious About Words
Copyright © Houghton Mifflin Harcourt Publishing Company

Pretest/Posttest Administration

Unit 3, Lesson 15

Pretest/Posttest Administration
Curious About Words

Grade K

Copy and distribute **Pretest/Posttest** pages 120–121. Also see directions, page 1.

Day 1–Day 2: Words About Night

1. **darkness** Which picture shows a time of **darkness**?
   - ○ [people hiking]
   - ● [night scene]
   - ○ [kids playing catch]

2. **silence** Which picture shows a place where there is **silence** before something begins?
   - ○ [race track]
   - ○ [pet store]
   - ● [movie theater]

3. **sky** Which picture shows something you can see in the **sky**?
   - ● [cloud]
   - ○ [tree]
   - ○ [rock]

4. **star** Which picture shows a **star**?
   - ● [shape with five points]
   - ○ [a round shape]
   - ○ [a square shape]

Day 3–Day 4: Words About Seeing

5. **look** Which picture shows someone who might need to **look** for something that is lost?
   - ○ [children napping]
   - ● [child in messy room]
   - ○ [child with flowers]

6. **noticed** Which picture shows a person who **noticed** the weather?
   - ○ [boy making sandwich]
   - ○ [girl setting table]
   - ● [girl looking out window]

7. **saw** Which picture shows a bus that someone **saw** go by?
   - ● [family missing bus]
   - ○ [children waiting for bus]
   - ○ [bus by itself]

8. **spy** Which picture shows a hen that can **spy** tracks?
   - ○ [hen frosting cake]
   - ○ [hen with pig]
   - ● [hen looking at tracks]

Unit 4, Lesson 16

Copy and distribute **Pretest/Posttest** pages 122–123. Also see directions, page 1.

Grade K

Pretest/Posttest Administration
Curious About Words

Day 1–Day 2: Words About Water

1. **emptied** Which picture shows something that must be **emptied**?
   - 🔴 [tub]
   - ○ [oar]
   - ○ [soap]

2. **ocean** Which picture shows the **ocean**?
   - 🔴 [water scene]
   - ○ [mountain scene]
   - ○ [tree]

3. **pond** Which picture shows a **pond**?
   - ○ [grassy scene]
   - ○ [skier on mountain]
   - 🔴 [water with frog]

4. **river** Which picture shows a **river**?
   - ○ [water in a park fountain]
   - 🔴 [moving water]
   - ○ [rain]

5. **stream** Which picture shows a **stream**?
   - 🔴 [moving water]
   - ○ [water in a fish tank]
   - ○ [girls at pool]

Day 3–Day 4: Words About Science

6. **kit** Which picture shows something you might find in a tool **kit**?
   - ○ [cooking pot]
   - ○ [iron]
   - 🔴 [hammer]

7. **magnifying** Which picture shows a person using a **magnifying** glass?
   - ○ [girl playing miniature golf]
   - 🔴 [man looking at tracks]
   - ○ [girl holding glass]

8. **observation** Which picture shows children making an **observation**?
   - 🔴 [boys watching birds]
   - ○ [boys on seesaw]
   - ○ [girl and boy playing]

9. **scientist** Which picture shows a **scientist**?
   - ○ [man scrubbing floor]
   - 🔴 [person using microscope]
   - ○ [boy eating]

10. **studied** Which picture shows people who **studied** something?
    - ○ [people standing]
    - ○ [boy with sad face]
    - 🔴 [girl and boy with map]

Curious About Words
Copyright © Houghton Mifflin Harcourt Publishing Company

Pretest/Posttest Administration

Unit 4, Lesson 17

Pretest/Posttest Administration
Curious About Words

Grade K

Copy and distribute **Pretest/Posttest** pages 124–125. Also see directions, page 1.

Day 1–Day 2: Words About Nature

1. **branches** Which picture shows animals that live in **branches**?
   - ○ [seals]
   - ● [owls and squirrels]
   - ○ [ducks]

2. **environment** Which picture shows a child in an **environment**?
   - ○ [girl standing]
   - ○ [boy in jacket]
   - ● [boy in a room]

3. **insects** Which picture shows **insects**?
   - ● [grasshopper, ant, caterpillar]
   - ○ [birds and prairie dog]
   - ○ [fish]

4. **leaves** Which picture shows **leaves**?
   - ○ [acorns]
   - ○ [seashells]
   - ● [branch with small things on it]

5. **soil** Which picture shows how people can use **soil**?
   - ● [boy planting seeds]
   - ○ [girl building snowman]
   - ○ [people in rowboat]

Day 3–Day 4: Words About Nature

6. **breeze** Which picture shows something people use to make a **breeze**?
   - ● [fan]
   - ○ [rain in puddle]
   - ○ [balloon]

7. **cloud** Which picture shows a **cloud** in the sky?
   - ○ [airplane]
   - ○ [ice cube]
   - ● [rain coming down]

8. **exploration** Which picture shows people enjoying an **exploration**?
   - ○ [children trading coins]
   - ● [people hiking]
   - ○ [ballet dancers]

9. **field** Which picture shows a place with a **field**?
   - ○ [bedroom]
   - ● [farm]
   - ○ [city scene]

10. **plant** Which picture shows a **plant**?
    - ○ [ladybug]
    - ○ [eggs]
    - ● [flower]

Unit 4, Lesson 18

Pretest/Posttest Administration
Curious About Words
Grade K

Copy and distribute **Pretest/Posttest** pages 126–127. Also see directions, page 1.

Day 1–Day 2: Words About Places

1. **here** Which picture shows how to get from **here** to there?
   - ○ [photo album]
   - ○ [stamps]
   - ● [map]

2. **high** Which picture shows something that looks **high**?
   - ○ [kids playing on the ground]
   - ● [building]
   - ○ [sheep walking]

3. **land** Which picture shows something that people ride only on **land**?
   - ● [motorcycle]
   - ○ [plane]
   - ○ [rowboat]

4. **places** Which picture shows **places** where you can buy food?
   - ○ [food items]
   - ○ [money]
   - ● [market]

5. **sand** Which picture shows a place where you could find lots of **sand** to play in?
   - ○ [pool]
   - ● [beach]
   - ○ [bedroom]

Day 3–Day 4: Words About Numbers

6. **five** Which picture shows **five** marbles?
   - ● [5 marbles in bag]
   - ○ [3 marbles in bag]
   - ○ [7 marbles in bag]

7. **four** Which picture shows **four** fish?
   - ○ [2 fish in bowl]
   - ○ [1 fish in bowl]
   - ● [4 fish in bag]

8. **one** Which picture shows **one** apple?
   - ○ [2 apples on plate]
   - ○ [3 apples in bag]
   - ● [1 apple]

9. **three** Which picture shows **three** balloons?
   - ● [girl with 3 balloons]
   - ○ [girl with 4 balloons]
   - ○ [girl with 2 balloons]

10. **two** Which picture shows **two** paint cans?
    - ○ [4 paint cans]
    - ● [2 paint cans]
    - ○ [3 paint cans]

Unit 4, Lesson 19

Grade K

Pretest/Posttest Administration
Curious About Words

Copy and distribute **Pretest/Posttest** pages 128–129. Also see directions, page 1.

Day 1–Day 2: Words About Hiking

1. **bring** Which picture shows something you would **bring** to school?
   - ○ [chalkboard]
   - ● [crayons]
   - ○ [desk]

2. **carry** Which picture shows how a person can **carry** something?
   - ○ [girl tossing ring]
   - ● [man carrying bureau]
   - ○ [man scrubbing floor]

3. **follow** Which picture shows animals that **follow** one another?
   - ● [ducklings and mother]
   - ○ [pig and goat]
   - ○ [dog and squirrel]

4. **see** Which picture shows something that helps some people **see** better?
   - ● [eyeglasses]
   - ○ [watch]
   - ○ [hug]

5. **walk** Which picture shows how a person can **walk**?
   - ○ [girl standing]
   - ○ [boy playing]
   - ● [boy moving]

Day 3–Day 4: Words That Tell Where

6. **above** Which picture shows something that is **above** someone?
   - ○ [children with cat]
   - ○ [children seated at table]
   - ● [girl with kite]

7. **across** Which picture shows something that cars can drive **across**?
   - ○ [fence]
   - ● [bridge]
   - ○ [tunnel]

8. **behind** Which picture shows something that is **behind** a boy?
   - ● [backpack with boy]
   - ○ [boy reaching for glove]
   - ○ [boy sharing drawings]

9. **below** Which picture shows an animal that lives **below** the ground?
   - ○ [fish]
   - ● [bird with worm]
   - ○ [caterpillar]

10. **location** Which picture shows you the **location** of the bus?
    - ○ [children on bus]
    - ○ [bus]
    - ● [people getting off bus at stores]

Curious About Words
Copyright © Houghton Mifflin Harcourt Publishing Company

Pretest/Posttest Administration

Unit 4, Lesson 20

Pretest/Posttest Administration
Curious About Words
Grade K

Copy and distribute **Pretest/Posttest** pages 130–131. Also see directions, page 1.

Day 1–Day 2: Words About Travel

1. **away** Which picture shows people who are going **away**?
   - ○ [children at tables]
   - ● [car leaving on trip]
   - ○ [people eating]

2. **country** Which picture shows a place to find a **country**?
   - ○ [dartboard]
   - ○ [calendar]
   - ● [map]

3. **go** Which picture shows someone getting ready to **go** somewhere?
   - ● [woman with bag]
   - ○ [children on swings]
   - ○ [children at school]

4. **journey** Which picture shows how someone might take a **journey**?
   - ○ [girl sitting]
   - ● [train]
   - ○ [boys on seesaw]

5. **world** Which picture shows the **world**?
   - ● [Earth]
   - ○ [fish under the sea]
   - ○ [garden plot]

Day 3–Day 4: Words About Time

6. **always** Which picture shows something people **always** need to go to a movie?
   - ● [ticket]
   - ○ [popcorn]
   - ○ [vest]

7. **never** Which picture shows an animal that **never** flies?
   - ○ [parrot]
   - ○ [bee]
   - ● [tiger]

8. **once** Which picture shows something people might do **once** each day?
   - ○ [girl climbing rock]
   - ● [boy in bathtub]
   - ○ [boy riding camel]

9. **whenever** Which picture shows something people need **whenever** it rains?
   - ● [umbrella]
   - ○ [mop]
   - ○ [soccer ball]

10. **years** Which picture shows a cake for someone who is six **years** old?
    - ○ [birthday cake with 3 candles]
    - ● [birthday cake with 6 candles]
    - ○ [birthday cake with 8 candles]

Unit 5, Lesson 21

Grade K

Pretest/Posttest Administration
Curious About Words

Copy and distribute **Pretest/Posttest** pages 132–133. Also see directions, page 1.

Day 1–Day 2: Words That Tell How Much

1. **all** Which picture shows **all** the outdoor clothes you need to play in snow?
   - ○ [boots]
   - ○ [coat]
   - ● [boots, coat, hat, and mittens]

2. **many** Which picture shows **many** hats?
   - ● [6 hats]
   - ○ [1 hat]
   - ○ [2 hats]

3. **more** Which picture shows **more** animals?
   - ● [group of animals, including a cow, a lion, a monkey]
   - ○ [bear]
   - ○ [bat]

4. **most** Which picture shows the **most** kites?
   - ○ [2 kites]
   - ● [6 kites]
   - ○ [4 kites]

5. **some** Which picture shows **some** children?
   - ○ [girl dancing]
   - ○ [boy with a baseball bat]
   - ● [a group of children]

Day 3–Day 4: Words About Friends

6. **friend** Which picture shows a child with a **friend**?
   - ● [boy and girl building sandcastle]
   - ○ [girl playing jacks alone]
   - ○ [boy on a bike]

7. **happy** Which picture shows a child who looks **happy**?
   - ● [girl dancing]
   - ○ [girl in a coat]
   - ○ [boy holding basketball]

8. **like** Which picture shows something people do when they want to show that they **like** each other?
   - ○ [children reading]
   - ● [children with arms around each other]
   - ○ [children walking]

9. **play** Which picture shows how friends might **play** together?
   - ○ [children arguing]
   - ○ [children writing]
   - ● [children playing in a puddle]

10. **share** Which picture shows something children usually **share** at a birthday party?
    - ● [birthday cake]
    - ○ [pile of birthday presents]
    - ○ [knapsack]

Unit 5, Lesson 22

Copy and distribute **Pretest/Posttest** pages 134–135. Also see directions, page 1.

Grade K

Pretest/Posttest Administration
Curious About Words

Day 1–Day 2: Words to Describe Animals

1. **different** A cat has four legs. Which picture shows an animal that has a **different** number of legs from a cat?
   - ○ [dog]
   - ● [hen]
   - ○ [cow]

2. **shaped** Which picture shows something that is **shaped** like a circle?
   - ○ [kite]
   - ○ [picture frame]
   - ● [balloon]

3. **size** Which picture shows the animal that is smallest in **size**?
   - ○ [duck]
   - ○ [horse]
   - ● [mouse]

4. **tough** Which picture shows something that is **tough**?
   - ● [football]
   - ○ [pillow]
   - ○ [flowers]

5. **weaker** Which picture shows an animal that is **weaker** than a dog?
   - ○ [elephant]
   - ● [bird]
   - ○ [bear]

Day 3–Day 4: Words About How Things Move

6. **come** Which picture shows someone who has **come** to the party?
   - ○ [girl setting table]
   - ● [children at the table]
   - ○ [girl getting dishes]

7. **hop** Which picture shows something a person could **hop** over?
   - ○ [clouds and sun]
   - ○ [a car]
   - ● [dog's food dish]

8. **pull** Which picture shows something a child can **pull**?
   - ● [a wagon]
   - ○ [a tree]
   - ○ [a house]

9. **reach** Which picture shows a boy who tries to **reach**?
   - ● [boy stretching arm up to shelf]
   - ○ [boy sitting on steps]
   - ○ [boy standing]

10. **turned** Which picture shows something that can be **turned** around?
    - ○ [house]
    - ● [bus]
    - ○ [mountains]

Unit 5, Lesson 23

Pretest/Posttest Administration
Curious About Words

Grade K

Copy and distribute **Pretest/Posttest** pages 136–137. Also see directions, page 1.

Day 1–Day 2: Words That Tell Where

1. **down** Which picture shows someone or something going **down**?
   - ○ [children running]
   - ● [boy on slide]
   - ○ [plane going into sky]

2. **into** Which picture shows apples that were put **into** something?
   - ○ [apples on a plate]
   - ● [pail of apples]
   - ○ [apples on a tree]

3. **off** Which picture shows someone who is **off** a bike?
   - ○ [girl with bike]
   - ○ [boy with bike]
   - ● [boy with bike]

4. **out** Which picture shows something that is **out** of its box?
   - ● [open box with ball next to it]
   - ○ [open box with ball inside it]
   - ○ [empty box]

5. **outside** Which picture shows something that is **outside**?
   - ○ [kitchen]
   - ● [playground]
   - ○ [bedroom]

Day 3–Day 4: Words About Size

6. **equal** Which picture shows the children holding an **equal** number of marbles?
   - ○ [children holding marbles, one with more than other]
   - ● [children holding marbles, each with 5]
   - ○ [children holding marbles, one with more than other]

7. **height** Which picture shows the way you would measure to find out the **height** of something?
   - ● [lamp with line up and down]
   - ○ [sofa with line across]
   - ○ [scale]

8. **inch** Which picture shows something that could be about an **inch** long?
   - ○ [truck]
   - ○ [shoe]
   - ● [paperclip]

9. **length** Which picture shows something you need to know the **length** of before you decide to buy it?
   - ○ [bag of apples]
   - ○ [baseball]
   - ● [pair of shoes]

10. **measurement** Which picture shows a **measurement**?
    - ○ [group of pencils]
    - ● [shoe]
    - ○ [thread]

Unit 5, Lesson 24

Grade K

Pretest/Posttest Administration
Curious About Words

Copy and distribute **Pretest/Posttest** pages 138–139. Also see directions, page 1.

Day 1–Day 2: Words About How Good Something Is

1. **better** Which picture shows something that is **better** for you to eat than cookies?
   - ○ [pie]
   - ○ [cake]
   - ● [apple]

2. **good** Look at each child's face. Which picture shows someone who might say, "This is a **good** day!"?
   - ○ [boy sitting on steps]
   - ○ [children skating]
   - ● [girl ice skating]

3. **great** Which picture shows someone who is having a **great** time?
   - ○ [girl in room]
   - ○ [boy reading quietly]
   - ● [boy showing excitement]

4. **pretty** Which picture shows something that you might call **pretty**?
   - ○ [mop]
   - ● [coat]
   - ○ [fly]

5. **wonderful** Which picture shows something **wonderful** happening?
   - ○ [boys grabbing a coat]
   - ● [child with present]
   - ○ [boy lifting heavy box]

Day 3–Day 4: Words About Speaking

6. **question** Which picture shows a child who might have a **question**?
   - ● [boy in group]
   - ○ [girl sleeping]
   - ○ [children laughing]

7. **retell** Which picture shows something you could **retell**?
   - ● [book/story]
   - ○ [teddy bear]
   - ○ [clock]

8. **said** Which picture best shows who might have **said** something?
   - ○ [child sleeping]
   - ● [boy with pet dish]
   - ○ [teddy bear]

9. **speech** Which picture shows the part of the body you use for **speech**?
   - ○ [ear]
   - ○ [eye]
   - ● [mouth]

10. **told** Which picture shows a child who is being **told** something?
    - ○ [boy with balloon]
    - ● [two children together]
    - ○ [girl with horse]

Curious About Words
Copyright © Houghton Mifflin Harcourt Publishing Company

Pretest/Posttest Administration

Unit 5, Lesson 25

Copy and distribute **Pretest/Posttest** pages 140–141. Also see directions, page 1.

Grade K

Pretest/Posttest Administration
Curious About Words

Day 1–Day 2: Words About Effort

1. **again** If you do something for the first time, and you do that same thing **again,** how many times have you done it?
   - ○ [numeral 0]
   - ○ [numeral 1]
   - ● [numeral 2]

2. **make** Which picture shows something you can **make**?
   - ● [sandwich]
   - ○ [bananas]
   - ○ [bird]

3. **try** Which picture shows something that would be all right for a five-year-old to **try** to do?
   - ● [swim]
   - ○ [lift something heavy]
   - ○ [drive]

4. **use** Which picture shows a way to **use** a crayon?
   - ○ [crayons in a box]
   - ● [drawing something]
   - ○ [crayon]

5. **want** Which picture shows something a person would **want**?
   - ○ [a broken vase]
   - ● [a friend]
   - ○ [broken eggs]

Day 3–Day 4: Words About What Is Yours

6. **his** Which picture goes with this sentence: "Those are **his** bananas"?
   - ○ [bananas in a store]
   - ○ [children sharing bananas]
   - ● [boy with bananas]

7. **our** Which picture shows someone who might say, "**our** hats"?
   - ● [children with hats]
   - ○ [girls, one with a hat]
   - ○ [girl with hat]

8. **own** Which picture shows something that might be your **own**?
   - ○ [moon/stars]
   - ● [shoes]
   - ○ [plane]

9. **their** Which picture shows **their** feelings?
   - ○ [sad boy]
   - ○ [happy girl]
   - ● [smiling children]

10. **your** Which picture shows someone who might say, "I like **your** hat"?
    - ○ [gardener with hat]
    - ○ [girl with hat]
    - ● [girls making hats]

Unit 6, Lesson 26

Copy and distribute **Pretest/Posttest** pages 142–143. Also see directions, page 1.

Grade K

Pretest/Posttest Administration
Curious About Words

Day 1–Day 2: Words About Shopping

1. **buy** Which picture shows someone who is about to **buy** something?
   - ○ [mother and child]
   - ● [girl with glove]
   - ○ [teacher and artwork]

2. **money** Which picture shows **money**?
   - ○ [kite with price tag]
   - ● [bills and coins]
   - ○ [bag of marbles]

3. **open** The door into the store was **open**. Which picture shows something that you could **open**?
   - ○ [bike]
   - ○ [rug]
   - ● [window]

4. **sell** Which picture shows something people **sell** to each other?
   - ○ [being friends]
   - ○ [moon]
   - ● [vegetables]

5. **spend** Which picture shows someone who might be asking, "What did I **spend** today"?
   - ● [man with wallet]
   - ○ [boy with clock]
   - ○ [girl with block]

Day 3–Day 4: Words About Other Names for People

6. **he** Which picture shows a person who would be called **he**?
   - ○ [girl]
   - ● [man]
   - ○ [woman]

7. **I** Which picture shows who or what would use the word **I** when talking?
   - ● [girl]
   - ○ [turtle]
   - ○ [yo-yo]

8. **they** Circle the picture that goes with this sentence: "**They** are standing in the rain."
   - ● [people in rain]
   - ○ [rain]
   - ○ [girl in rain]

9. **we** Which picture shows someone who could say, "**We** are playing with the dog"?
   - ○ [dog with boy]
   - ○ [dogs with girl]
   - ● [dog with boys]

10. **you** Which picture shows who or what could be called **you**?
    - ● [boy]
    - ○ [blocks]
    - ○ [book]

Curious About Words
Copyright © Houghton Mifflin Harcourt Publishing Company

Unit 6, Lesson 27

Grade K

Pretest/Posttest Administration
Curious About Words

Copy and distribute **Pretest/Posttest** pages 144–145. Also see directions, page 1.

Day 1–Day 2: Words About Learning

1. **education** Which picture best shows children who are getting an **education**?
   - ○ [children running]
   - ○ [child playing]
   - ● [classroom with teacher]

2. **know** Which picture shows something children would not **know**?
   - ○ [how to swim]
   - ○ [how to ride a bike]
   - ● [how to drive]

3. **learning** Which picture shows someone **learning** how to do something?
   - ○ [girl alone on bike]
   - ● [girl on bike with help]
   - ○ [man on bike]

4. **think** Which picture shows something a person can **think** about but not do?
   - ○ [reading]
   - ○ [camping]
   - ● [jumping over a house]

5. **thought** Which picture shows where a person would have a **thought**?
   - ○ [in a hand]
   - ● [in the head]
   - ○ [in the feet]

Day 3–Day 4: Words About Thoughts and Thinking

6. **believe** Which picture shows something you would **believe** if someone told you it happened?
   - ○ [lion in dentist's chair]
   - ● [dog chasing cat]
   - ○ [animals reading]

7. **idea** Which picture shows who or what could have a good **idea**?
   - ○ [soup]
   - ● [person]
   - ○ [cup]

8. **knowledge** Which picture shows a good place to get **knowledge**?
   - ○ [closet]
   - ○ [cupboard]
   - ● [classroom]

9. **remembered** Which picture shows how you might feel if you **remembered** to do your chores?
   - ● [happy]
   - ○ [sad]
   - ○ [angry]

10. **understand** Think about walking by a table, a child, and a teddy bear. Which one of them would **understand** you if you smiled as you walked by?
    - ○ [table]
    - ● [child]
    - ○ [bear]

Curious About Words
Copyright © Houghton Mifflin Harcourt Publishing Company

Pretest/Posttest Administration

Unit 6, Lesson 28

Copy and distribute **Pretest/Posttest** pages 146–147. Also see directions, page 1.

Grade K

Pretest/Posttest Administration
Curious About Words

Day 1–Day 2: Words About Art

1. **draw** Which picture shows how someone can **draw**?
   - ● [child at a desk]
   - ○ [child with a ruler]
   - ○ [child with scissors]

2. **hang** We sometimes **hang** our artwork in school. Which picture shows something else that you can **hang**?
   - ○ [house]
   - ○ [fish tank]
   - ● [coat]

3. **paint** Which picture shows how someone can **paint**?
   - ○ [child with paper]
   - ● [child with brush]
   - ○ [man with book]

4. **pictures** Which picture shows a teacher with some **pictures**?
   - ○ [teacher sitting]
   - ○ [teacher watching]
   - ● [teacher standing]

5. **show** Which of these people wants to **show** something right now?
   - ○ [girl asleep]
   - ● [boy with drawing]
   - ○ [girl hiding eyes]

Day 3–Day 4: Words About Places

6. **California** Which picture shows where you could look to find **California**?
   - ● [map]
   - ○ [bag of groceries]
   - ○ [school building]

7. **city** Which picture shows a **city**?
   - ● [tall buildings]
   - ○ [houses]
   - ○ [a barn]

8. **museum** Which picture shows something you do at a **museum**?
   - ○ [play soccer]
   - ○ [play basketball]
   - ● [look at pictures]

9. **school** Which picture shows what it is like to be at **school**?
   - ○ [child with pail]
   - ● [children listening]
   - ○ [child in kitchen]

10. **station** Which picture shows someone at a **station**?
    - ● [man by tracks]
    - ○ [man running]
    - ○ [child in garden]

Curious About Words — Pretest/Posttest Administration

Unit 6, Lesson 29

Copy and distribute **Pretest/Posttest** pages 148–149. Also see directions, page 1.

Day 1–Day 2: Words About Friends

1. **both** Circle the picture that best goes with this sentence: "We are **both** running."
   - ○ [two girls]
   - ● [man and woman]
   - ○ [three girls]

2. **buddy** Which picture shows someone with a **buddy**?
   - ● [two boys]
   - ○ [boy]
   - ○ [girl]

3. **partner** Which picture shows someone who has a **partner**?
   - ● [children building]
   - ○ [children in school]
   - ○ [boy watering]

4. **together** Which picture shows something being done **together**?
   - ○ [writing]
   - ● [soccer]
   - ○ [scrubbing]

5. **with** Circle the picture that goes with this sentence: "I'm going **with** you."
   - ○ [children walking]
   - ○ [man and car]
   - ● [two girls]

Day 3–Day 4: Words About People

6. **audience** Which picture has an **audience** in it?
   - ● [person singing]
   - ○ [children playing]
   - ○ [man painting]

7. **entertainer** Which picture shows an **entertainer**?
   - ○ [girls playing]
   - ○ [man in office]
   - ● [child with puppet]

8. **family** Which picture shows a **family**?
   - ○ [man]
   - ○ [children and cat]
   - ● [adults and kids]

9. **father** Which picture shows a **father**?
   - ○ [woman]
   - ○ [man]
   - ● [man and kids]

10. **people** Which picture shows **people**?
    - ● [adults and children]
    - ○ [animals]
    - ○ [balls]

Unit 6, Lesson 30

Copy and distribute **Pretest/Posttest** pages 150–151. Also see directions, page 1.

Grade K

Pretest/Posttest Administration

Curious About Words

Day 1–Day 2: Words About a Party

1. **celebrate** Which picture shows how it feels to **celebrate** a birthday?
   - ○ [sad face]
   - ● [smiling face]
   - ○ [angry face]

2. **party** Circle the picture that goes with this sentence: "The table is ready for the **party**."
   - ● [table with gifts]
   - ○ [table and chairs]
   - ○ [table]

3. **photograph** Which picture shows what you would use to make a **photograph**?
   - ○ [pot]
   - ○ [paint]
   - ● [camera]

4. **surprised** Which picture shows something you would be **surprised** to see at school?
   - ○ [water fountain]
   - ● [ducks in classroom]
   - ○ [children with bus]

5. **wrapped** Which picture shows something that is **wrapped**?
   - ○ [boat]
   - ○ [crayons]
   - ● [box]

Day 3–Day 4: Words About Choices

6. **choices** Circle the picture that goes with this sentence: "There are good **choices** of fruit here."
   - ○ [banana]
   - ● [fruit at grocery store]
   - ○ [pear]

7. **decide** Which picture shows someone who needs to **decide** what to eat?
   - ● [boy with choices of fruit]
   - ○ [boy eating]
   - ○ [boy with ice cream cone]

8. **information** Which picture shows something you can use to get **information**?
   - ○ [cup]
   - ○ [pail]
   - ● [books]

9. **judge** Which picture shows one way to **judge** a drawing?
   - ○ [child drawing another child]
   - ● [teacher with drawings]
   - ○ [child drawing]

10. **or** Which picture goes with this sentence: "Do I want this one **or** that one"?
    - ○ [boy with empty arms]
    - ● [boy with banana and apple]
    - ○ [girl with teddy bear]

Name _____ Date _____

Words About Moms

Unit 1, Lesson 1
BLACKLINE MASTER 1–01

Pretest/Posttest
Curious About Words

1.

2.

3.

4.

Curious About Words
Copyright © Houghton Mifflin Harcourt Publishing Company

Grade K, Unit 1, Lesson 1

Name _____ Date _____

Unit 1, Lesson 1
BLACKLINE MASTER 1-02

Pretest/Posttest
Curious About Words

Words About a Family Visit

5.

6.

7.

8.

Curious About Words
Copyright © Houghton Mifflin Harcourt Publishing Company

93

Grade K, Unit 1, Lesson 1

93

Name _____ Date _____

Unit 1, Lesson 2
BLACKLINE MASTER 1-03

Pretest/Posttest
Curious About Words

Words About Being Safe in Water

1.

2.

3.

4.

Curious About Words
Copyright © Houghton Mifflin Harcourt Publishing Company

94

Grade K, Unit 1, Lesson 2

Name _____   Date _____

Words About Feelings

Unit 1, Lesson 2
BLACKLINE MASTER 1-04

Pretest/Posttest
Curious About Words

5.

6.

7.

8.

Curious About Words
Copyright © Houghton Mifflin Harcourt Publishing Company

Grade K, Unit 1, Lesson 2

Name _____ Date _____

Unit 1, Lesson 3
BLACKLINE MASTER 1–05

Pretest/Posttest
Curious About Words

Words About Size

1.

2.

3.

4.

Curious About Words
Copyright © Houghton Mifflin Harcourt Publishing Company

Grade K, Unit 1, Lesson 3

Name _____ Date _____

Unit 1, Lesson 3
BLACKLINE MASTER 1-06

Pretest/Posttest
Curious About Words

Words About Time

5.

6.

7.

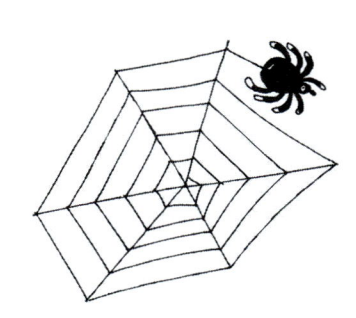

8.

Curious About Words

97

Grade K, Unit 1, Lesson 3

Name _____ Date _____

Unit 1, Lesson 4
BLACKLINE MASTER 1-07

Pretest/Posttest
Curious About Words

Words About Helping Out

1.

2.

3.

4.

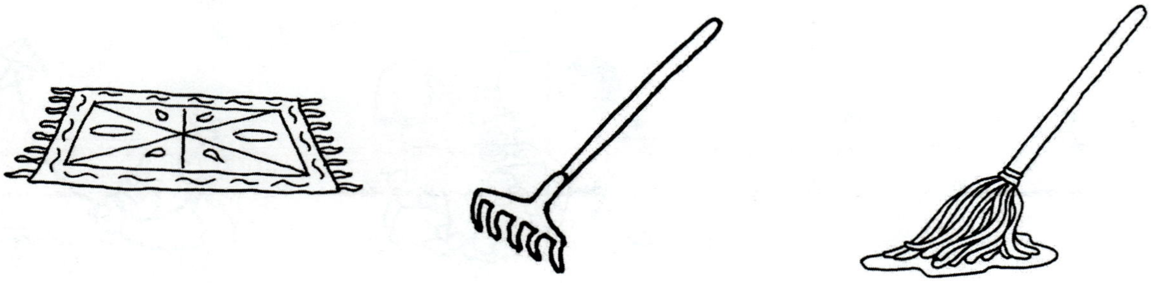

Curious About Words
Copyright © Houghton Mifflin Harcourt Publishing Company

98

Grade K, Unit 1, Lesson 4

Name _____ Date _____

Unit 1, Lesson 4
BLACKLINE MASTER 1-08

Words About Jobs

Pretest/Posttest
Curious About Words

5.

6.

7.

8.

Curious About Words

Grade K, Unit 1, Lesson 4

Name _____ Date _____

Unit 1, Lesson 5
BLACKLINE MASTER 1-09

Pretest/Posttest
Curious About Words

Words About Bugs

1.

2.

3.

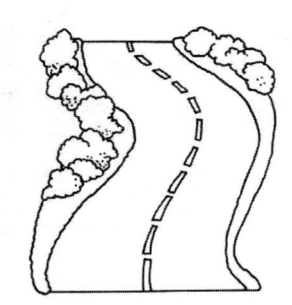

4.

Curious About Words
Copyright © Houghton Mifflin Harcourt Publishing Company

100

Grade K, Unit 1, Lesson 5

100

Name _____ Date _____

Words About a Visit to the Doctor

Unit 1, Lesson 5
BLACKLINE MASTER 1–10

Pretest/Posttest
Curious About Words

5.

6.

7.

8.

Curious About Words

101

Grade K, Unit 1, Lesson 5

Copyright © Houghton Mifflin Harcourt Publishing Company

Name _____ Date _____

Words About Sounds

Unit 2, Lesson 6
BLACKLINE MASTER 2–11

Pretest/Posttest
Curious About Words

1.

2.

3.

4.

Curious About Words
Copyright © Houghton Mifflin Harcourt Publishing Company

102

Grade K, Unit 2, Lesson 6

102

Name _____ Date _____

Unit 2, Lesson 6
BLACKLINE MASTER 2-12

Pretest/Posttest
Curious About Words

Words About Our Senses

5.

6.

7.

8.

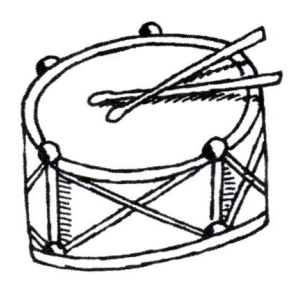

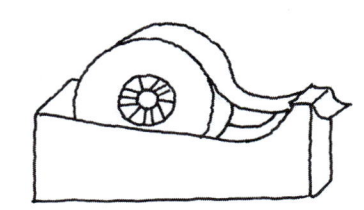

Curious About Words
Copyright © Houghton Mifflin Harcourt Publishing Company

103

Grade K, Unit 2, Lesson 6

Name _____ Date _____

Words About Sounds

Unit 2, Lesson 7
BLACKLINE MASTER 2-13

Pretest/Posttest
Curious About Words

1.

2.

3.

4.

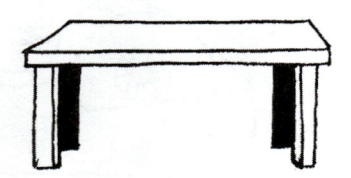

Curious About Words
Copyright © Houghton Mifflin Harcourt Publishing Company

Grade K, Unit 2, Lesson 7

Name _____ Date _____

Unit 2, Lesson 7
BLACKLINE MASTER 2–14

Pretest/Posttest
Curious About Words

Words About Communication

5.

6.

7.

8.

Curious About Words   105   Grade K, Unit 2, Lesson 7
Copyright © Houghton Mifflin Harcourt Publishing Company

Name _____ Date _____

Unit 2, Lesson 8
BLACKLINE MASTER 2–15

Pretest/Posttest
Curious About Words

Words About Moving Your Body

1.

2.

3.

4.

Curious About Words
Copyright © Houghton Mifflin Harcourt Publishing Company

106

Grade K, Unit 2, Lesson 8

106

Name _____ Date _____

Unit 2, Lesson 8
BLACKLINE MASTER 2–16

Pretest/Posttest
Curious About Words

Words About Animal Actions

5.

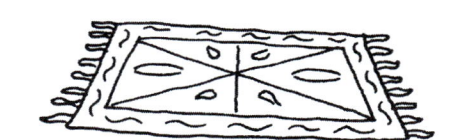

6.

7.

8.

Curious About Words

107

Grade K, Unit 2, Lesson 8

Copyright © Houghton Mifflin Harcourt Publishing Company

Name _____ Date _____

Unit 2, Lesson 9
BLACKLINE MASTER 2-17

Pretest/Posttest
Curious About Words

Words About Asking Questions

1.

2.

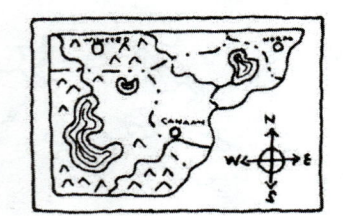

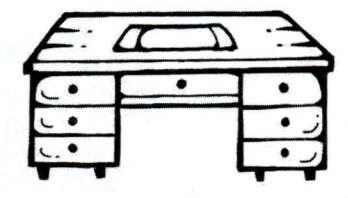

3.

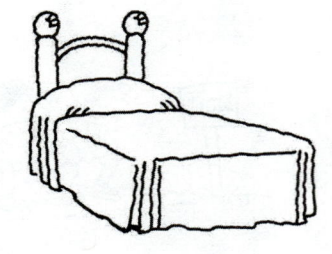

4.

Name _____ Date _____

Words About Building Things

Unit 2, Lesson 9
BLACKLINE MASTER 2–18

Pretest/Posttest
Curious About Words

5.

6.

7.

8.

Curious About Words
Copyright © Houghton Mifflin Harcourt Publishing Company

109

Grade K, Unit 2, Lesson 9

109

Name _____ Date _____

Unit 2, Lesson 10
BLACKLINE MASTER 2–19

Pretest/Posttest
Curious About Words

Words About What People Are Like

1.

2.

3.

4.

Curious About Words
Copyright © Houghton Mifflin Harcourt Publishing Company

110

Grade K, Unit 2, Lesson 10

Name _____ Date _____

Words That Tell Where

Unit 2, Lesson 10
BLACKLINE MASTER 2-20

Pretest/Posttest
Curious About Words

5.

6.

7.

8.

Curious About Words
Copyright © Houghton Mifflin Harcourt Publishing Company

Grade K, Unit 2, Lesson 10

Name _____ Date _____

Unit 3, Lesson 11
BLACKLINE MASTER 3–21

Pretest/Posttest
Curious About Words

Words About Migration

1.

2.

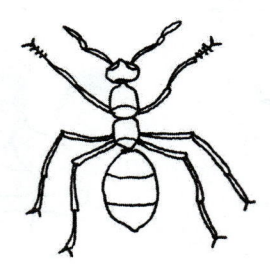

3.

4.

Curious About Words
Copyright © Houghton Mifflin Harcourt Publishing Company

112

Grade K, Unit 3, Lesson 11

112

Name _____ Date _____

Unit 3, Lesson 11
BLACKLINE MASTER 3-22

Words About Seasons

Pretest/Posttest
Curious About Words

5.

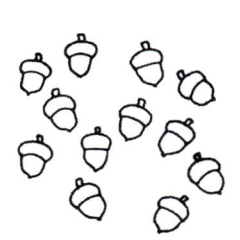

6.

7.

8.

Curious About Words 113 Grade K, Unit 3, Lesson 11

Name _____ Date _____

Words About Storms

Unit 3, Lesson 12
BLACKLINE MASTER 3-23

Pretest/Posttest
Curious About Words

1.

2.

3.

4.

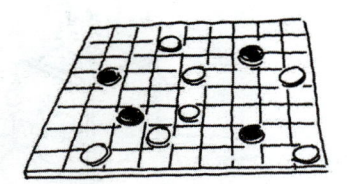

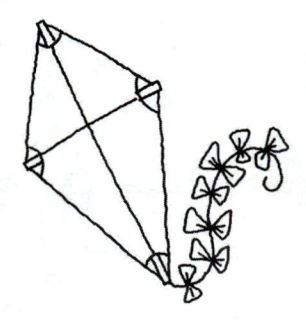

Curious About Words
Copyright © Houghton Mifflin Harcourt Publishing Company

114

Grade K, Unit 3, Lesson 12

114

Name _____ Date _____

Unit 3, Lesson 12
BLACKLINE MASTER 3–24

Pretest/Posttest
Curious About Words

Words About School

5.

6.

7.

8.

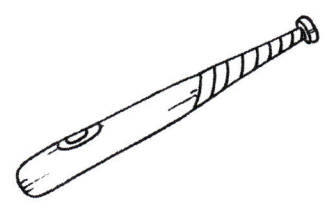

Curious About Words

115

Grade K, Unit 3, Lesson 12

Copyright © Houghton Mifflin Harcourt Publishing Company

115

Name _____ Date _____

Words About Colors

Unit 3, Lesson 13
BLACKLINE MASTER 3-25

Pretest/Posttest
Curious About Words

1.

2.

3.

4.

Curious About Words
Copyright © Houghton Mifflin Harcourt Publishing Company

116

Grade K, Unit 3, Lesson 13

116

Name _____ Date _____

Unit 3, Lesson 13
BLACKLINE MASTER 3-26

Pretest/Posttest
Curious About Words

Words for Describing Animals

5.

6.

7.

8.

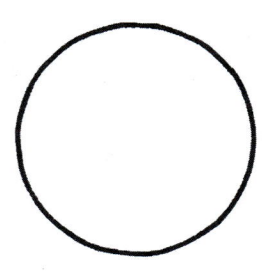

Curious About Words
Copyright © Houghton Mifflin Harcourt Publishing Company

117

Grade K, Unit 3, Lesson 13

117

Name _____ Date _____

Unit 3, Lesson 14
BLACKLINE MASTER 3-27

Pretest/Posttest
Curious About Words

Words About Distance

1.

2.

3.

4.

Name _____   Date _____

Unit 3, Lesson 14
BLACKLINE MASTER 3-28

Pretest/Posttest
Curious About Words

Words About Actions

5.

6.

7.

8.

Curious About Words
Copyright © Houghton Mifflin Harcourt Publishing Company

119

Grade K, Unit 3, Lesson 14

119

Name _____ Date _____

Words About Night

Unit 3, Lesson 15
BLACKLINE MASTER 3-29

Pretest/Posttest
Curious About Words

1.

2.

3.

4.

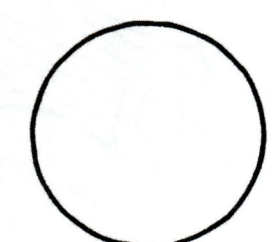

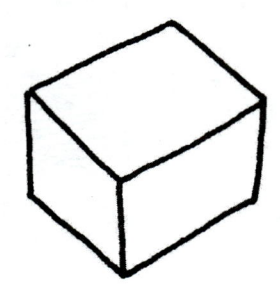

Curious About Words
Copyright © Houghton Mifflin Harcourt Publishing Company

120

Grade K, Unit 3, Lesson 15

Name _____ Date _____

Words About Seeing

Unit 3, Lesson 15
BLACKLINE MASTER 3-30

Pretest/Posttest
Curious About Words

5.

6.

7.

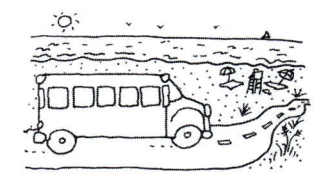

8.

Curious About Words
Copyright © Houghton Mifflin Harcourt Publishing Company

121

Grade K, Unit 3, Lesson 15

121

Name _____ Date _____

Unit 4, Lesson 16
BLACKLINE MASTER 4-31

Pretest/Posttest
Curious About Words

Words About Water

1.

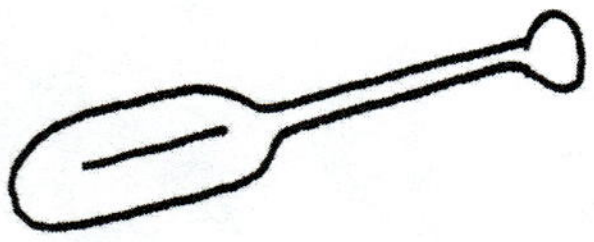

2.

3.

4.

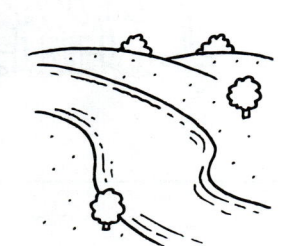

5.

Curious About Words
Copyright © Houghton Mifflin Harcourt Publishing Company

Grade K, Unit 4, Lesson 16

Name _____ Date _____

Unit 4, Lesson 16
BLACKLINE MASTER 4-32

Words About Science

Pretest/Posttest
Curious About Words

6.

7.

8.

9.

10.

Curious About Words
Copyright © Houghton Mifflin Harcourt Publishing Company

Grade K, Unit 4, Lesson 16

Name _____ Date _____

Words About Nature

Unit 4, Lesson 17
BLACKLINE MASTER 4-33

Pretest/Posttest
Curious About Words

1.

2.

3.

4.

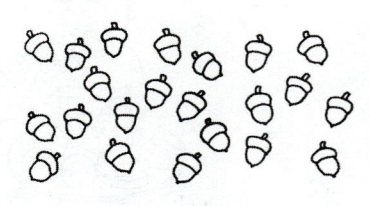

5.

Curious About Words
Copyright © Houghton Mifflin Harcourt Publishing Company

Grade K, Unit 4, Lesson 17

Name _____ Date _____

Unit 4, Lesson 17
BLACKLINE MASTER 4-34

Words About Nature

Pretest/Posttest
Curious About Words

6.

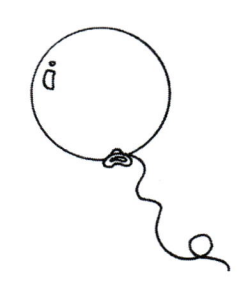

7.

8.

9.

10.

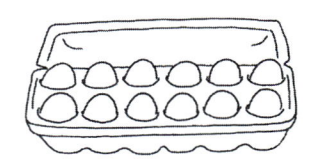

Curious About Words
Copyright © Houghton Mifflin Harcourt Publishing Company

Grade K, Unit 4, Lesson 17

Name _____ Date _____

Words About Places

Unit 4, Lesson 18
BLACKLINE MASTER 4–35

Pretest/Posttest
Curious About Words

1.

2.

3.

4.

5.

Curious About Words
Copyright © Houghton Mifflin Harcourt Publishing Company

Grade K, Unit 4, Lesson 18

Name _____ Date _____

Unit 4, Lesson 18
BLACKLINE MASTER 4-36

Words About Numbers

Pretest/Posttest
Curious About Words

6.

7.

8.

9.

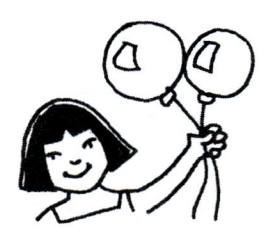

10.

Curious About Words

Copyright © Houghton Mifflin Harcourt Publishing Company

Grade K, Unit 4, Lesson 18

Name _____ Date _____

Unit 4, Lesson 19
BLACKLINE MASTER 4-37

Words About Hiking

Pretest/Posttest
Curious About Words

1.

2.

3.

4.

5.

Curious About Words
Copyright © Houghton Mifflin Harcourt Publishing Company

Grade K, Unit 4, Lesson 19

Name _____ Date _____

Unit 4, Lesson 19
BLACKLINE MASTER 4-38

Words That Tell Where

Pretest/Posttest
Curious About Words

6.

7.

8.

9.

10.

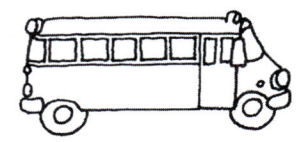

Curious About Words

Copyright © Houghton Mifflin Harcourt Publishing Company

Grade K, Unit 4, Lesson 19

Name _____ Date _____

Unit 4, Lesson 20
BLACKLINE MASTER 4-39

Pretest/Posttest
Curious About Words

Words About Travel

1.

2.

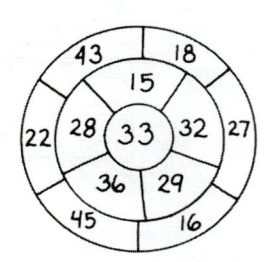

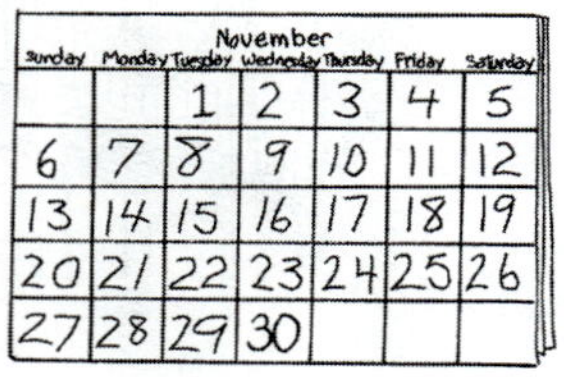

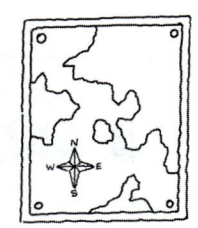

3.

4.

5.

Curious About Words
Copyright © Houghton Mifflin Harcourt Publishing Company

Grade K, Unit 4, Lesson 20

Name _____ Date _____

Unit 4, Lesson 20
BLACKLINE MASTER 4–40

Words About Time

Pretest/Posttest
Curious About Words

6.

7.

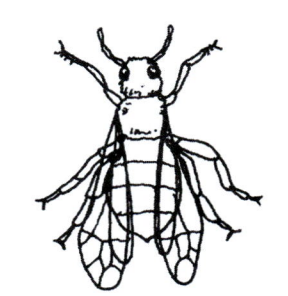

8.

9.

10.

Curious About Words
Copyright © Houghton Mifflin Harcourt Publishing Company

131

Grade K, Unit 4, Lesson 20

131

Name _____ Date _____

Unit 5, Lesson 21
BLACKLINE MASTER 5-41

Pretest/Posttest
Curious About Words

Words That Tell How Much

1.

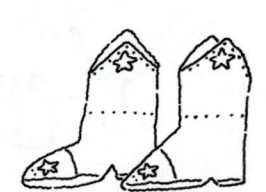

2.

3.

4.

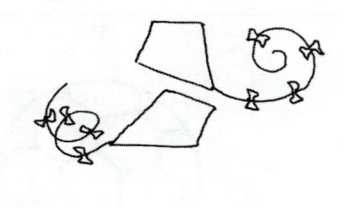

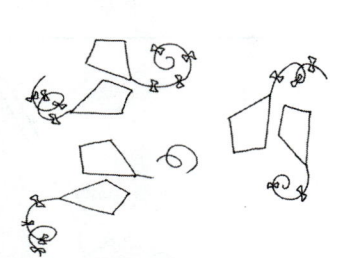

5.

Curious About Words
Copyright © Houghton Mifflin Harcourt Publishing Company

132

Grade K, Unit 5, Lesson 21

Name _____ Date _____

Words About Friends

Unit 5, Lesson 21
BLACKLINE MASTER 5-42

Pretest/Posttest
Curious About Words

6.

7.

8.

9.

10.

Curious About Words
Copyright © Houghton Mifflin Harcourt Publishing Company

Grade K, Unit 5, Lesson 21

Name _____ Date _____

Words to Describe Animals

Unit 5, Lesson 22
BLACKLINE MASTER 5-43

Pretest/Posttest
Curious About Words

1.

2.

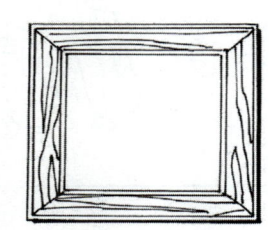

3.

4.

5.

Name _____ Date _____

Unit 5, Lesson 22
BLACKLINE MASTER 5-44

Pretest/Posttest
Curious About Words

Words About How Things Move

6.

7.

8.

9.

10.

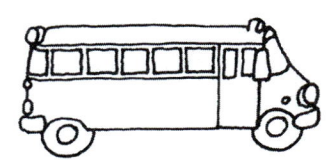

Curious About Words
Copyright © Houghton Mifflin Harcourt Publishing Company

Grade K, Unit 5, Lesson 22

Name _____ Date _____

Unit 5, Lesson 23
BLACKLINE MASTER 5–45

Words That Tell Where

Pretest/Posttest
Curious About Words

1.

2.

3.

4.

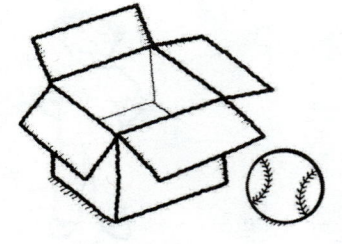

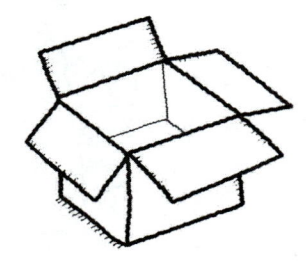

5.

Curious About Words
Copyright © Houghton Mifflin Harcourt Publishing Company

Grade K, Unit 5, Lesson 23

Name _____ Date _____

Unit 5, Lesson 23
BLACKLINE MASTER 5-46

Pretest/Posttest
Curious About Words

Words About Size

6.

7.

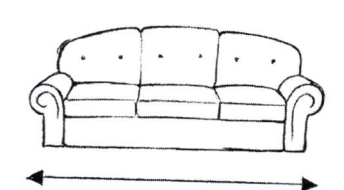

8.

9.

10.

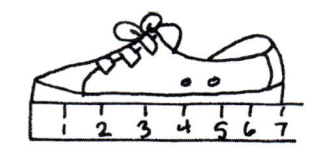

Curious About Words
Copyright © Houghton Mifflin Harcourt Publishing Company

137

Grade K, Unit 5, Lesson 23

Name _____ Date _____

Unit 5, Lesson 24
BLACKLINE MASTER 5–47

Pretest/Posttest
Curious About Words

Words About How Good Something Is

1.

2.

3.

4.

5.

Curious About Words
Copyright © Houghton Mifflin Harcourt Publishing Company

Grade K, Unit 5, Lesson 24

Name _____ Date _____

Unit 5, Lesson 24
BLACKLINE MASTER 5–48

Words About Speaking

Pretest/Posttest
Curious About Words

6.

7.

8.

9.

10.

Curious About Words
Copyright © Houghton Mifflin Harcourt Publishing Company

Grade K, Unit 5, Lesson 24

Name _____ Date _____

Words About Effort

Unit 5, Lesson 25
BLACKLINE MASTER 5–49

Pretest/Posttest
Curious About Words

1. 0   1   2

2.

3.

4.

5.

Curious About Words
Copyright © Houghton Mifflin Harcourt Publishing Company

140

Grade K, Unit 5, Lesson 25

Name _____ Date _____

Unit 5, Lesson 25
BLACKLINE MASTER 5-50

Pretest/Posttest
Curious About Words

Words About What Is Yours

6.

7.

8.

9.

10.

Curious About Words
Copyright © Houghton Mifflin Harcourt Publishing Company

Grade K, Unit 5, Lesson 25

Name _____ Date _____

Unit 6, Lesson 26
BLACKLINE MASTER 6–51

Words About Shopping

Pretest/Posttest
Curious About Words

1.

2.

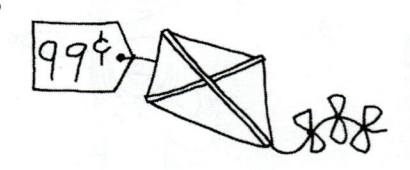

3.

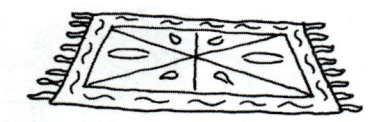

4.

5.

Curious About Words
Copyright © Houghton Mifflin Harcourt Publishing Company

Grade K, Unit 6, Lesson 26

Name _____ Date _____

Unit 6, Lesson 26
BLACKLINE MASTER 6-52

Pretest/Posttest
Curious About Words

Words About Other Names for People

6.

7.

8.

9.

10.

Curious About Words
Copyright © Houghton Mifflin Harcourt Publishing Company

Grade K, Unit 6, Lesson 26

Name _____ Date _____

Unit 6, Lesson 27
BLACKLINE MASTER 6–53

Words About Learning

Pretest/Posttest
Curious About Words

1.

2.

3.

4.

5.

Curious About Words
Copyright © Houghton Mifflin Harcourt Publishing Company

Grade K, Unit 6, Lesson 27

Name _____ Date _____

Unit 6, Lesson 27
BLACKLINE MASTER 6–54

Words About Thoughts and Thinking

Pretest/Posttest
Curious About Words

6.

7.

8.

9.

10.

Curious About Words
Copyright © Houghton Mifflin Harcourt Publishing Company

145

Grade K, Unit 6, Lesson 27

Name _____ Date _____

Words About Art

Unit 6, Lesson 28
BLACKLINE MASTER 6–55

Pretest/Posttest
Curious About Words

1.

2.

3.

4.

5.

Curious About Words
Copyright © Houghton Mifflin Harcourt Publishing Company

Grade K, Unit 6, Lesson 28

Name _____ Date _____

Unit 6, Lesson 28
BLACKLINE MASTER 6-56

Words About Places

Pretest/Posttest
Curious About Words

6.

7.

8.

9.

10.

Curious About Words
Copyright © Houghton Mifflin Harcourt Publishing Company

147

Grade K, Unit 6, Lesson 28

147

Name _____   Date _____

Unit 6, Lesson 29
BLACKLINE MASTER 6–57

Pretest/Posttest
Curious About Words

Words About Friends

1.

2.

3.

4.

5.

Curious About Words
Copyright © Houghton Mifflin Harcourt Publishing Company

Grade K, Unit 6, Lesson 29

Name _____   Date _____

Words About People

Unit 6, Lesson 29
BLACKLINE MASTER 6-58

Pretest/Posttest
Curious About Words

6.

7.

8.

9.

10.

Curious About Words
Copyright © Houghton Mifflin Harcourt Publishing Company

Grade K, Unit 6, Lesson 29

Name _____ Date _____

Unit 6, Lesson 30
BLACKLINE MASTER 6-59

Pretest/Posttest
Curious About Words

Words About a Party

1.

2.

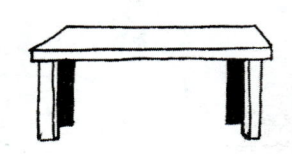

3.

4.

5.

Curious About Words
Copyright © Houghton Mifflin Harcourt Publishing Company

150

Grade K, Unit 6, Lesson 30

Name _____ Date _____

Words About Choices

Unit 6, Lesson 30
BLACKLINE MASTER 6-60

Pretest/Posttest
Curious About Words

6.

7.

8.

9.

10.

Curious About Words
Copyright © Houghton Mifflin Harcourt Publishing Company

151

Grade K, Unit 6, Lesson 30

151

Word List

Unit 1

Lesson 1 (pp. T2–T3)

Words About Moms	Words About a Family Visit
her	cousin
mother	crowded
parent	food
she	visit

Lesson 2 (pp. T4–T5)

Words About Being Safe in Water	Words About Feelings
attention	curious
prevent	furious
safety	impatient
water	shocked

Lesson 3 (pp. T6–T7)

Words About Size	Words About Time
enormous	sometimes
large	soon
little	suddenly
small	until

Lesson 4 (pp. T8–T9)

Words About Helping Out	Words About Jobs
chores	busy
help	jobs
responsibility	services
wash	work

Lesson 5 (pp. T10–T11)

Words About Bugs	Words About a Visit to the Doctor
gathered	break
hill	healed
tunnel	illness
worker	injury

Unit 2

Lesson 6 (pp. T12–T13)

Words About Sounds
- applause
- bursting
- pounding
- screaming

Words About Our Senses
- noises
- scent
- smooth
- vibration

Lesson 7 (pp. T14–T15)

Words About Sounds
- call
- hear
- sing
- sound

Words About Communication
- laughs
- message
- talks
- voice

Lesson 8 (pp. T16–T17)

Words About Moving Your Body
- bend
- motion
- muscles
- rest

Words About Actions
- curled
- escaping
- race
- sneaked

Lesson 9 (pp. T18–T19)

Words About Asking Questions
- how
- what
- where
- why

Words About Building Things
- build
- create
- shovels
- tool

Lesson 10 (pp. T20–T21)

Words About What People Are Like
- character
- funny
- kind
- quiet

Words That Tell Where
- around
- between
- over
- under

Word List • 153

Unit 3

Lesson 11 (pp. T22–T23)

Words About Migration
- beaks
- bird
- distance
- fly

Words About Seasons
- blooming
- cold
- grow
- temperature

Lesson 12 (pp. T24–T25)

Words About Storms
- damage
- dangerous
- shake
- wind

Words About School
- paper
- stories
- teacher
- write

Lesson 13 (pp. T26–T27)

Words About Colors
- blue
- brown
- green
- yellow

Words About Describing Animals
- color
- eyes
- head
- trait

Lesson 14 (pp. T28–T29)

Words About Distance
- area
- deepest
- far
- near

Words About Actions
- climbing
- eat
- landing
- live

Lesson 15 (pp. T30–T31)

Words About Night
- darkness
- silence
- sky
- stars

Words About Seeing
- look
- noticed
- saw
- spy

154 • Curious About Words

Unit 4

Lesson 16 (pp. T32–T33)

Words About Water
- emptied
- ocean
- pond
- river
- stream

Words About Science
- kit
- magnifying
- observation
- scientist
- studied

Lesson 17 (pp. T34–T35)

Words About Nature
- branches
- environment
- insects
- leaves
- soil

More Words About Nature
- breeze
- cloud
- exploration
- field
- plant

Lesson 18 (pp. T36–T37)

Words About Places
- here
- high
- land
- places
- sand

Words About Numbers
- one
- two
- three
- four
- five

Lesson 19 (pp. T38–T39)

Words About Hiking
- bring
- carry
- follow
- see
- walk

Words That Tell Where
- above
- across
- behind
- below
- location

Lesson 20 (pp. T40–T41)

Words About Travel
- away
- country
- go
- journey
- world

Words About Time
- always
- never
- once
- whenever
- years

Unit 5

Lesson 21 (pp. T42–T43)

Words That Tell How Much	Words About Friends
all	friend
many	happy
more	like
most	play
some	share

Lesson 22 (pp. T44–T45)

Words to Describe Animals	Words About How Things Move
different	come
shaped	hop
size	pull
tough	reach
weaker	turned

Lesson 23 (pp. T46–T47)

Words That Tell Where	Words About Size
down	equal
into	height
off	inch
out	length
outside	measurement

Lesson 24 (pp. T48–T49)

Words About How Good Something Is	Words About Speaking
better	question
good	retell
great	said
pretty	speech
wonderful	told

Lesson 25 (pp. T50–T51)

Words About Effort	Words About What Is Yours
again	his
make	our
try	own
use	their
want	your

Unit 6

Lesson 26 (pp. T52–T53)

Words About Shopping
- buy
- money
- open
- sell
- spend

Words About Other Names for People
- he
- I
- they
- we
- you

Lesson 27 (pp. T54–T55)

Words About Learning
- education
- know
- learning
- think
- thought

Words About Thoughts and Thinking
- believe
- idea
- knowledge
- remembered
- understand

Lesson 28 (pp. T56–T57)

Words About Art
- draw
- hang
- paint
- pictures
- show

Words About Places
- California
- city
- museum
- school
- station

Lesson 29 (pp. T58–T59)

Words About Friends
- both
- buddy
- partner
- together
- with

Words About People
- audience
- entertainer
- family
- father
- people

Lesson 30 (pp. T60–T61)

Words About a Party
- celebrate
- party
- photograph
- surprised
- wrapped

Words About Choices
- choices
- decide
- information
- judge
- or

Research Sources for Words Taught

Dale, E., & O'Rourke, J. (1981). *The living word vocabulary.* Chicago: World Book/Childcraft International.

Hiebert, E.H. (2005). WordZones™ based on "In pursuit of an effective, efficient vocabulary curriculum for elementary students," in E. H. Hiebert & M. Kamil (Eds.) *Teaching and learning vocabulary: bringing research to practice.* Mahwah, NJ: Lawrence Erlbaum Associates.

Marzano, Robert (2004). *Building background knowledge for academic achievement.* Alexandria, VA: Association for Supervision and Curriculum Development.

Templeton, S. (2006). "Derivationally related word families among the most frequently occurring words in English." (Unpublished)

Zeno, S.M, Ivens, S.H., Millard, R.T., & Duvvuri, R. (1995). *The educator's word frequency guide.* New York: Touchstone Applied Science Associates, Inc.